A Capful of Wind

Useless information for aspiring skippers

Written and Illustrated
by
Monica Matterson

Oxford eBooks

A Capful of Wind
This edition Copyright © 2014 by Oxford eBooks Ltd.

Illustrations and Story Copyright © 2012 by Monica Matterson

The right of the author to be identified as the author of this work
has been asserted in accordance with the Copyright, Designs and
Patents Act 1988.

All rights reserved. No part of this publication may be reproduced,
stored in a retrieval system, or transmitted, in any form or by
any means, electronic, mechanical, photocopying, recording or
otherwise, without the prior permission of the copyright owners.

ISBN 978-1-908387-96-7

This book is also avaialble as
an eBook and in hardback

ISBN 978-1-908387-75-2 (ePUB)
ISBN 978-1-908387-74-5 (MOBI)

Book and eBook designed and published
by Oxford eBooks Ltd.

www.oxford-ebooks.com
enquiries@oxford-ebooks.com

Acknowledgements

My thanks go to Mr. W.S. Hudson (Bill) who in our early learning years was the principal of the New Parks Community Project and formed the New Parks Cruising Association, which we joined. Being over one hundred miles to the sea in any direction, this was quite a unique enterprise and covered tuition from dinghy sailing through the R.Y.A. specifications up to Ocean and Instructors courses. If it were not for his and his fellow tutor's enthusiasm, encouragement and good humoured bullying I could not have had the fun and experiences that follow.

More than a little gratitude must also be given to the many other student crew members who unwittingly provided the raw material for the anecdotes. Many of these fellows now have their own boats and are teaching the next generation of 'would be sailors'.

An unfortunate sign of the times is that the Community Project now ceases to exist, but a few old stalwarts still manage to meet monthly to 'swing the lamp' reminisce old times and plan more passages.

Last but not least, thank you Sam for your patience with reading, re-reading, typing, and your unsuccessful efforts to teach me to understand a computer and also for taking me sailing for so many years.

Dedications

This collection of old drawings is strung together with a light-hearted look at the joys and miseries of taking the necessary steps to becoming a qualified Yachtmaster. It is thus dedicated to all unsuspecting newcomers to the sea with aspirations of becoming a competent sailor. Happy cruising.

Chapter One

Testing the Water

Knowing absolutely nothing about the qualities to look for when buying a boat, our first venture, in 1968, into something that floats, was 14 foot of solid mahogany — a clinker-built hulk. For £100 it came with a geriatric Seagull engine, oars, and sails for its Gunter rig, trailer, and bailer. We named it *Trilobite* for its likeness to a pre-historic sea creature.

When re-varnished and gleaming, we took it with pride to a local Yacht Club on the river Soar, near to where we then lived. They were most friendly, and helped us launch and push off. This was adventure indeed! By the time the gaff pole had dropped onto our heads, and we had poked a few new channels through the reeds, it was noticed that the insidious ingress of the brackish Soar through the dried-out caulking was now well over our ankles. Our two boys, Paul, 16 years, and John, 14, bailed frantically as we rowed sheepishly back to the slipway.

Trilobite, now twice its weight, took us and six smirking club members considerable patience and effort to set it back on the trailer.

"Nice to see you, do come back again sometime — when you have an Enterprise!" said the courteous Commodore.

Launching and un-launching was always a problem. But once afloat it comfortably held two adults, four children and a dog, although progress was frustratingly slow. This limitation was made very clear one day on Loch Long in Scotland. With a picnic packed, Sam, myself and the two boys were wafting slowly up the middle of the Loch towards Loch Goil when peace was broken by the roar of a powerful engine.

"Look Dad!" said Paul, "Do you think he's seen us?" Looking to starboard, there was an impressive tidal wave almost hiding the naval patrol boat which was bearing down on us at a worrisome rate of knots. With dignity, we held our course and speed of one and a half knots, waiting for the crunch. It swooped round and suddenly stopped, slopping a few gallons of Loch over the lunch basket. Whilst still clinging, white-knuckled, to the strake, a large booming tannoy instructed us to get into the side.

"You are in line with the submarine torpedo practice!" The U.S. Navy possibly muttered a few of their cuss words as they watched us ineptly trying to comply with their demands. Wanting to sound as efficient as possible we went through the 'ready about' and 'Lee ho' bit — and the breeze died! The Seagull engine coughed mockingly at the futile attempts to start it whilst the patrol boat hovered impatiently nearby until we had slowly lollopped closer to shore. The practice torpedo was clearly seen just below the surface of the water as it trundled past half a cable to starboard. The boys thought it highly amusing; we were not so sure but managed to laugh when the shock wore off. I wonder what was entered in the Naval log book?!

Trilobite was sold back to the boatyard whence it was purchased shortly after that.

"You are in line with the submarine torpedo practice!"

Chapter Two

Dabbling

Several years passed and the boys had left home before Sam casually revealed that he had always wanted to build a boat; but until now, bringing up a family and its demands had taken first priority. "That will keep him quiet in the shed." I thought, after the initial surprise wore off!

On learning that he meant a yacht about 35 foot long, not a dinghy, it put a different face on the matter, so I could not refrain from making a comment or two "If you work at the same rate as you do when putting up a shelf or painting a ceiling, by the time it is finished you will be too old to sail it!" and "How will you get it out of the back garden without knocking down the garage?" With that, we began touring around boatyards looking for a fibre-glass hull to fit out, still not knowing what configuration we wanted or even what choices there were.

To get into nautical mode, we chartered a skippered 32 foot Hilliard for a week out of Salcombe. The boat was old and traditional, not very comfortable, with coffin-like bunks and a temperamental loo. The skipper, too, was of the old school — no using the engine, no marinas, and the Gin locked in a cupboard! Each night the anchorage was miles from civilisation, and on the one occasion that we escaped in the dinghy, moonlight mud-wrestling under the Tamar Bridge was not what was anticipated for an evening's entertainment! "But I thought you had looked up low water time…"

One thing that did impress us was, when the fog came down across Lyme bay, our skipper disappeared below, did some sums, then told us what time we should pass the Mew stone. He was right! It suddenly appeared so close you could almost touch it. Not much knowledge of sailing was gained on this trip but we learnt to appreciate the use of navigation and tide tables.

A summer passed trial sailing Roggers and Banjers up the Towey, Contests up the Orwell and Moodys on the Hamble, contemplating also an Oyster shell at Ipswich, all of which became very confusing as it dawned that the most sturdy and comfortable craft did not sail so well as the less opulent ones.

Meanwhile, another chartered week with a skipper was organised, this time on a 28 foot Jaguar sloop in Menorca. The skipper, Danny, was a young French lad on holiday from the Swedish Navy with a guitar, happy outlook, and a policy that says "Every day is a celebration!" The other crew-member was also a young bachelor, who turned up rather drunk at 4 a.m. "Great!" we griped, "What are we in for? We are here to get away from younger elements of our own!"

There was no need to have worried. On the second day, being mistakenly deemed efficient enough for a night sail to Mallorca, I was left on watch alone with instructions to wake the skipper if anything untoward happened. There were no navigational aids or autohelm on this frisky little craft, so after nearly an hour on an impish tiller, concentration wandered off into the mesmeric phosphorescence. A couple of unexpected gybes seemed to pass unnoticed, it was the second 360 degrees turn that brought up a bleary-eyed Danny to ask about the "yacht with the waltzing gait"!

All went well for a spell after he told me how to line up a star on the shroud. Keeping a look-out at all times as one should, I next saw all these lights in the distance and to me, that could only mean one thing — Mallorca! "Land Ho!" seemed the accepted thing to shout, - "I can see a village!" I was delighted that we had arrived so quickly I thought, as we sailed nearer. Danny emerged again, just in time to see my *village* pass across our bows, a large ocean liner! I was grateful to be relieved of that first watch.

The next few days were idyllic, Danny played his guitar and sang to the dolphins, whilst Rick and ourselves tried to improve on sailing technique - like how to un-jam a riding turn when doing six knots towards the cliff face.

Evenings were definitely more fun than the last trip, especially when anchored in 8 foot of crystal clear turquoise water of Cala Galdana or Portals instead of tidal cocoa. Putting towels and clothes into a sailbag, tossing it into the dinghy, we could then swim ashore pushing it along and dress on the beach.

This being the mid-70's, ladies wore long dresses, and the men always a tie, so there was a bit of titivating and comb-borrowing to do before tipping the dinghy over our gear. Not realising that we had been a spectator sport, it came as a surprise to hear a round of applause from the balconies of the overlooking villas as this assorted crew strode across the beach and into the nearest tall hotel, only to go up in the lift to the foyer out of their front door and across the road to an unpretentious *Carlo's Caff* for dinner.

Returning later by the same method, the glow of Vino Tinto was outshone by the spectacular glow of the phosphorescent algae which illuminated every kick with dazzling green lights as we swam.

A week with these two lively lads had been a tonic, and perhaps we had learnt that such a tender boat was not for us, so the search goes on.

Across in Burnham-on-Crouch we watched Mr Prior building his sturdy 'Coasters', motor-sailers, but there were no second-hand ones about then, and a new one was out of the question. Having only gone down for the weekend, as many boatyards as possible were visited in that area. It rained non-stop, we were tired, confused, fed up and ready to go home, when something just prompted us to look across to a decrepit notice-board. The 'For Sale' sheets were rain-dribbled, smudged and unreadable. Rickety wooden steps led up to what looked like a tarred shed, and the lights were still on, so we decided there was time for a last enquiry, "It so happens we have just got a 32 foot Macwester Wight, bilge keel, ketch waiting to go into next month's magazine - just two years old, sir!" We gaped, having never even considered anything as new as this, but allowed ourselves to be led into a very dark shed to behold it, on chocks, in the gloom.

Still not knowing what we really wanted, we gave it a brief once-over, trying to make intelligent observations. The crunch had come! – "Would you like to make an offer, sir?" Having absolutely no idea, thought it might be best to go off and worry about it in comfort. A borrowed magazine showed that anything similar was then, in 1976, in the region of £12,000 — "Out of the question — forget it!"

The next day, chafing, pondering and calculating, it was

agreed that we would offer a cheeky £9,000 and if refused, then the search starts again. I was frightened, and even more so when our audacious offer was tentatively made and surprisingly, accepted, and the knees turned to jelly.

The next hurdle would be the bank manager, and being Sunday, nothing more could be done. After a restless night at the local inn, Sam rang his bank, delivered the normal morning courtesies, then "How would you like to buy a boat? It's very nice – sir!" Sir, all too quickly, agreed!

Cirdan, named after a character from *Lord of the Rings*, was now ours, together with an attic full of warps, shackles, sails, life-jackets, and pile of other equipment for mysterious purposes, as yet, unknown to us. Slowly, the day's events were realised when driving home in a daze of euphoria mixed with apprehension!

There followed several weekends of enthusiastic cleaning, anti-fouling, and varnishing aided by family and many new friends we didn't know we had, all hoping to be asked to go sailing. Being the smallest of us, I was, naturally, invited to scrape off the barnacles between the bilge keels and paint inside the cockpit lockers, making the initial enthusiasm sometimes difficult to maintain whilst reminding myself that, soon we would be sailors!

Equipment for mysterious purposes

Chapter Three

Waking the Dragon

The weekend came, at last, when the geriatric crane crawled down the road like some pre-historic monster, followed by a small group of curious onlookers, one of which was heard to say, as *Cirdan* dangled on its sling, "Wouldn't it be funny if they dropped it?"

"No. It would not, that's our boat!" I rapped back, and decided not to look until it had been swung round over the sea-wall and dumped onto the mud.

Six of us plothered out to sit on the deck drinking tea and trying to look casual while waiting for the tide to lift it off under the bemused gaze of the now greatly increased number of viewers.

Our mooring, we were told, was a quarter of a mile across the other side of the river, a large buoy with a ring on top, next but one to *Morning Cloud*, a then prestigious yacht — we were in good company!

The 36 hp. B.M.C. Captain diesel engine was kindly, and started immediately, so with great confidence sped off to pick up the buoy. What we didn't know was that the proper way to pick one up was to stem the tide and not to go with it, and with the tide running out at three knots it gave each of us a sporting chance to try and do better than the last whilst blaming everyone else for missing it. At last, it was secure; but, to try and prove that it was not just a fluke, thought it would be wise to go off and do it again for practise, since we still had plenty of time. "Perhaps if you attacked it from the other direction?" said a tentative little voice from one of the boys' girlfriend. So there happened the first lesson on our first day on the water.

The series of incidents which followed, now make us cringe with shame at those memories, but they make helpful reading for the would-be sailor as he pokes at his dragon, not knowing what he is about to stir up. A few of the more weathered veterans may empathise with events that they have been keeping quiet about for years!

Chapter Four

Are we having fun yet?

It was for a two week holiday in July that next we went down very excitedly, just the two of us, a box of provisions, and a small chart — it was going to be wonderful!

The *Seagull* engine behaved, we remembered to look which way the tide was running, and as the dinghy headed across the glassy calm river towards *Cirdan* on such a beautiful summer evening, we thought how lucky we were to have all this! Feet up, the newspaper, a gin and tonic at one's elbow and no kids! Such was the bliss in this rose-tinted evening calm.

The tide turned, I went below to begin groundwork on a Spaghetti Bolognese for supper, and shortly became aware that the boat was sneakily restless instead of standing still, and if I just held the spoon in the pan, the Bolognese stirred itself causing bewilderment between brain and stomach which I tried to ignore.

"GET ME OFF!"— The bosun of the Royal Burnham Yacht Club was very observant and responded at once to the frantic shouting and waving, possibly thinking that we were on fire by the fuss we made.

"Aaar, you'm a bit 'o wind o'er tide jes' now, she'll gow cum dark." Supper was abandoned and we ate on terra firma, and whilst there, thought it might be useful to apply for membership to the club in case of further problems. It also occurred to us that, in future, we might gauge meals and tides more conveniently. The next day, a light breeze and sunshine lured us cautiously from the mooring buoy not knowing that the customary practise was to leave your dinghy on it. The little tender flopped along dutifully astern, perhaps a bit too far behind, on the way seawards, which was a good two miles off.

A few wrong strings were pulled before the foresail went up, it filled, we cheered, and switched off the engine. The technicalities of yacht design were yet a mystery, so the fact that although our boat was a solid, safe, dependable tub, it had not occurred to us that it might need a force four to get it interested, nor had we remembered to fetch the Tide Tables.

Still slowly sailing within the confines of the estuary, between the moored boats, confidence soared, I was permitted to take the wheel. "Oh, the power!" Happening to glance behind, as I thought one should, I saw a trawler, F18, (I remember it well!) bearing down, quite quickly upon the stern. "Sam, look! What shall I do?"

"Hold your course and stop panicking" came the reply.

It took a few seconds for the message from the eyes to tell the brain that F18 was securely chained on her fore and aft mooring buoys, and *Cirdan* was now sailing sedately backwards, having lost the battle between the light wind and the fast-flooding tide.

Before brain had chance to tell muscles what to do about the situation, our lengthy dinghy painter had deftly wrapped itself round the trawler's forward chain, causing the equivalent of the Driving Test emergency stop.

For some reason, I thought that the problem could be

"Oops!" Kissing the buoy on the cheek

solved by scrambling aboard this malodorous, slimy rust-bucket, and attempt to poke it free with a boat-hook. Ours proved too short. F18's was three inches in diameter, twelve feet long, which propelled me across the fish-scaled deck like Sir Galahad at a tournament. I slipped on something nasty and narrowly missed being catapulted over the bow.

Being such an unwieldy hook, it took some time to unwind the dinghy from the chain, and Sam was getting a little peevish. The smirks and remarks from passing *yotties* pertaining to buckets of water and 'how to get rid of your wife', were getting too embarrassing, is that why he had turned away? Oblivious that I had now completed my mission, and put back the mighty boat-hook, he had drifted off too distracted to remember that there was a good 36 h.p. engine under him.

Composure regained, and now making better progress with the help of the mainsail bravely hoisted there, ahead, was the wide river mouth with the sea beyond.

The large, round, red and white middle-ground buoy was very *conspic* half a mile off.

When one has a choice of which side to pass it, you don't necessarily make the right one! Having remembered to note which way the tide was going and where the wind was coming from, there seemed plenty of time and space to leave this buoy to starboard. The closer it came, the more we doubted our choice - wrong! 'Tack!' Too slow, too late, *Cirdan* kissed the buoy gently on the cheek, nudged round it, *boing, boing, boing*, and dragged the dinghy over the top, and there was a good mile of open water on either side! Glad to see there were no boats near enough to see the latest clanger of these two berks at large who, by now, had seen

Joe - Last seen snaking along the path!

enough adventure for one day, when more lessons had been learnt.

Later that evening, during a therapy session at the inn, we fell in with a group of eager local fellows who had once crewed for Mr Heath and they would love to come for an evening sail with us. I'm not sure what they expected, but it certainly was not a slow, bumbling tub like *Cirdan*, which bore no resemblance whatever to *Morning Cloud!* Nor did we expect to be tacking for five miles up-river, "Lee-ho'ing" every few yards prompted by the flashing of the depth-finder, stirring up the mud and nudging the banks at each turn.

When the river narrowed to about twenty metres, they reluctantly gave in. The run back, being too tame to need their attention gave them the opportunity to seriously deplete our beer supplies now they had had their fun!

Not a lot was learnt from that evening, except, perhaps, not to ask them again.

Next, we met Joe. You have all seen this character, the be-whiskered old sea-dog who sits at the corner of the bar, trying to look interesting and waiting to be bought a drink. He said he would be happy to come tomorrow and show us a few tricks — for a free lunch and maybe a drop of Scotch! That's fine!

He arrived, as promised at 10 a.m., but first needed a 'wee dram' to get him going. So far, we had not ventured any further than that middle-ground buoy, so his suggestion of Brightlingsea sounded like an adventurous long voyage.

After ploughing a furrow in the mud when trying to recall the short-cut through the Ray Sand Channel, Joe needed another wee dram to get re-orientated.

Between regular draughts of Scotch he taught us how to neatly coil warps, bag the jib whilst still hanked on, moor up onto a pontoon, and that 'springs' were not the coiled pieces of metal that usually came to mind. That gave him a healthy appetite for lunch taken with another dram or two, with which he fell asleep, leaving us to find our own way back to Burnham.

He was last seen snaking along the path on a rusty old bicycle towards his green, tumbledown house-boat. Local gossip has it that he fell off into the mud three times before reaching home. Odd that we never saw him again!

That evening, we kept away from the pub. The sunset painted a spectacular canvas of reds, oranges, and violet over the sky and calm, peaceful waters — the end of a satisfying day.

Sometime during the night, something was gnawing into my sleep, a rumbling, a loud crack and the sound of torrential rain beating on the deck. Reluctantly rousing enough to realise that the rain was now dripping in from the open hatch over our bunks, I sat up to close it.

The simultaneous flash of lightning illuminated the dinghy, complete with outboard motor, as it flew in the air like a kite, and descended upside-down. "Oh, bother!" — or words to that effect woke up Sam, and we both scrambled out in our night-wear (such garments were worn in those days).

It is still not certain what sharp protrusion playfully clawed at the fly of Sam's pyjama trousers as he dashed down the deck, but the leg ripped from top to bottom, illuminating the 'full Monty' glistening in the lightning and driving rain. All I could do under the circumstance was to

However calm the evening seemed...

M. Matterson
1997.

Don't let go of the Seagull!

offer a few words of sympathy and encouragement as with the wet, torn leg flapping in the wind, he climbed down the boarding ladder to try and turn the dinghy upright.

By now, the waves were bucking it like a crazy horse, and there hung Sam, holding on with one hand and attempting to flip it over with the other whilst his dignity blew in the wind. At last it was righted, and he could climb into the dinghy to unscrew the outboard engine, in order to pass it up to me. This, too, was not as simple as we thought. With the Seagull cradled in both arms and the pyjama leg inexplicably wound round its propeller there was little to provide balance.

Having become just a little anxious by now, for some reason, I thought it sounded helpful to shout "Whatever you do, don't let go of it!" when the awkward burden threatened to lurch Sam overboard!

Now both engine and dinghy were safely tied down, shaking with fear and cold, dripping, and clutching a mug of cocoa we mulled over this ridiculous train of events which never should have happened. "Are we having fun yet?" I wondered! The brief moment of mirth was erased by the realisation of what a dangerous situation it could have been, no life-jackets or harnesses on, and no torch. What fools we are!!

Next day saw us shopping for serious oilskins, wellies, and harnesses. There were only two lifejackets, so, for now, courtesy would have to dictate who should wear them if we had company on board.

This week was Burnham Week, second only to Cowes Week. All the big boys were there including Mr Heath on *Morning Cloud* and his local crew, the ones who had given us the evening's entertainment on *Cirdan*.

Not wishing to get tangled up, or cause any vitriolic expletives among the racers, we thought it more diplomatic to sail to a vantage point and watch the events. 'Bearings' was still an unknown word, but you know how you somehow feel that things have moved? After re-anchoring five times, and losing concentration on the racing, we gave up.

Later, in the *White Hart*, the know-alls took delight in telling how they had noticed our difficulty anchoring, and other antics. We blamed it onto bad holding ground, but the locals knew better — "You need much more chain in that spot!" So far, we had assumed that only enough chain to reach the seabed was required! A quick glance to each other was enough warning to keep our mouths shut about that.

To avoid further aggravation to the racers, we plucked up courage to take ourselves off to Brightlingsea again. This stretch of coastline is almost featureless and bedevilled with sand and mud banks, and by the time you are far enough off-shore to avoid them, there is hardly anything to be seen in any direction.

There is a little white streak, though, — can't make it out — long way off yet, and Cirdan was cracking along, full sail at all of 5kts. towards it. On taking a curious look through the binoculars, the white streak became more obvious. "I shouldn't go over there, dear, they are seagulls walking about on a sandbank!" A few tacks later, disorientation takes over in the enveloping greyness, and the binoculars make black rings round the eyes with scouring 360 degrees hoping for a clue. At last, something! It looks like a silo. Silos are on farms, that looks promising, it must be land — Go for it!

An hour later, the *silo* was definitely closer, but still

indistinct. Consulting the one and only chart, looking for conspics on land, it was duly identified as *Rough's Tower*, serving no apparent purpose, several miles off Harwich! We did find Brightlingsea and enjoyed its old world charm for three days before summoning up enough bottle to make the passage back.

Sitting on deck, safely back on our buoy and watching the racers return, a very loud pompous voice proclaimed "Oh, Blast! Some bastard's pinched our mooring!" He sailed up, glowered, remonstrated, and insisted that he had paid somebody a handsome fee for the week on that buoy!

"Tough — it's ours!"

The same night, Mr Heath was upended from his dory by his victorious crew whilst landing at the Royal Corinthian Yacht Club. Burnham mud is black and sloppy — it did not improve his impeccable white trousers.

Determined to get his money's worth, and not be outdone, next day, the intruding yacht reached our moorings before us, and because he had either gone ashore or was hiding below, we had to look for another vacant one. Almost impossible in Burnham Week, so we were delighted to find one really close to town.

It was 4 a.m. My sleep had been disturbed, Sam was not in his bunk, and I could hear voices. He was on the stern, just shaking hands with a very anxious, superior - looking chap on the bow of his 27 foot sloop.

I made a cup of tea to help along the small-talk whilst waiting for the boats to swing into place on the tide. It seemed a very long wait. *Cirdan* was slow and reluctant and obviously on the wrong sized mooring and the eye-ball to eye-ball conversation became stilted. He began to look decidedly peevish, so we cast off and retreated to the end of the club pontoon, for the remainder of the night to enable him to catch up on his sleep or press his white trousers for the morning's race.

The holiday came to an end. At first, we were reasonably chuffed with the progress made in boat-handling, but then began reflecting on our serious lack of seamanship, knowledge, and respect for the sea with all its dangers — not to mention the numerous embarrassments. No, never, ever mention them again — best forgotten!

Something must be done; not everything can be gleaned from the little yellow and black 'Teach yourself' books, so how can we learn when we live so far from the sea? People are always glad of a chance to tell you what you should be doing, so, a short time later it was suggested that the largest sailing school in the country at that time, and also the furthest from the sea, was only ten miles away in Leicester. It catered for all stages from dinghy sailing up to Yachtmaster and Ocean level and evening classes began in September 1976.

Chapter Five

The lower learning curve

Thus it was that three would-be *yotties* enrolled at the New Parks Community Centre, dubbed 'Bill's Academy of Sailing'. Our eldest son, Paul, then twenty four years old, had decided to join in to keep an eye on what his old folks were up to next, as we were light-heartedly tutored by Tom, through boat parts, safety, and rules of the road. Navigation, under the sarcastic guidance of John, who's sharp eyes never missed an error, was an ordeal for me. Why did I always end up on the area of bench with the sink and dripping tap when trying to make an accurate running fix? And why did my family think it so amusing to slam the '*Reed's* shut as they passed it to me, after finding out tide times together? This made me slow and the butt of barbed remarks which left me feeling like a naughty schoolgirl. However, in spite of John's request that "The Matterson family will please NOT do this exam as a syndicate!" I managed quite well by myself in spite of the sink.

Practical assessments took place at Easter and Whitsuntide and any other possible weekend when candidates were offered a berth for a very modest fee in those days, for a taste of the real thing.

For the benefit of aspiring newcomers to the pleasures of cruising, I would like to pass on some of the knowledge we have gained through experiences of our own, in accordance with the R.Y.A teachings, but not necessarily in the manuals. One of the foremost aims on a practical week is to impress your skipper at every possible opportunity, pander to his most outrageous whims, kowtow, feed him well, have a ready answer to his questions, volunteer for everything, toady if you must but do not snore or leave your dirty socks about.

Hearing - to? (or three)

"Never mind chaps, only another 5 hours !"

Coastal 1. Competent Crew.

1. Making sail.

Before being able to raise the foresail, students must know how to 'bend on' the sheets, so, to avoid the wrath of an impatient to be off skipper by taking twenty minutes to tie a bowline, check that your rabbit runs round the correct tree before going back down its hole. Alternatively, you can take your own tea-towel with the knot design, and just happen to hang it on the guard-rail at a convenient height. This can save time and flummox in harbours like Yarmouth where the sightseers are watching your every move. If you wish to crib even more, there are tea-towels with flags, Beaufort Scale, and Recognition marks on them. You may have to offer to dry the dishes more often than at home, but remember, you are trying to impress the skipper, and for this week he is God!

2. Use of halyards.

Normally intended for raising and lowering of sails, and not for drying knickers, socks or other sundries on.

If the wrong one is selected to lower a sail, it will not go unnoticed, especially if the mainsail comes rattling down instead of the cruising chute or vice-versa.

3. Sailing a course. The points of sailing.

Tacking, Running, Gybing, Broad reaching, and Close hauled, Heaving-to and Beating.

4. Steering a course relative to the wind and also by compass.

These exercises can be interpreted in various ways.

Tacking

"I'm a lady !...."

Running

"Morning departure!"

Broad Reach

The age of chivalry is not quite dead!

Beating

Monica working for Costal !

Close Haul

Broad Reach

Ready About!

Anchoring

... he keeps shouting "Straight up and down !"

5. Anchoring and Mooring

Anchoring is usually undertaken by, at least five crew members, each eager to show the next chap how it should be done, whilst your skipper yells abuse from the helm. "What the ---- are you lot ----ing about at? Haven't you ever dropped a ---- anchor before? I want it straight up and down!"

It is prudent to check that the end of the anchor-chain, or warp, is attached to the boat before letting it all go, or you could spend an exhausting hour or two diving for it in the totally wrong place until 'Skip' has stopped crying.

Fingers must be kept well clear of the chain and bow-roller to be ready to make the appropriate gestures in reply to this foul abuse, or for blocking ears to same.

In choosing a mooring, other than in a marina, there are certain places to avoid.

Your image as a dashing *yottie* can be impaired if you have to cross the decks of a more sophisticated craft where the pink-rinsed poodles sit watching television, or the Doberman lurks near the patio doors, then a glowering lady wearing her *Marigold* gloves dashes out past the cut-glass vase of gladioli to rub out your footprints with a J-Cloth every time you walk across.

It is considered courteous to ask permission to moor alongside another boat, especially if it is larger and has more chromium than yours, although politeness is not always appreciated at 2 a.m. Sometimes you may be lucky enough to get some assistance, as we did after groping our way into Poole harbour one dirty night. Going aground at six knots and almost jettisoning three crewmen over the bow was not my fault, they should have noticed the unlit

Mooring up on trots

"Got it, skip!"

buoy or kept an eye on the novice who thought it a privilege to be handed the wheel for the first time. So, a bit of mud-shuffling, cursing and blame-shifting followed, and it was now too late for last orders at the *Crab and Ferret*.

"Mind if we come alongside?" we shouted to a vague shape leaning over the stern of a largish vessel.

"Wot?", the request was repeated. "Wot, ugh? Doh!"

Mooring up !
Bradwell marina, Essex 1978

"When we are nearer the pontoon, throw the rope, Pussikins darling."

"Throw the bloody rope woman!!"

"No need to shout, Tigsey Wigsey!"

Something had registered and he disappeared below, duly re-appearing with an obviously superior being who loudly summoned "All hands on deck!" whereupon, twenty, teenage youths made a bleary, but eager appearance, scattering about like a disturbed ant's nest. They tried to look busy, and their skipper was delighted with this unexpected exercise as we patiently endured his teaching process — mooring up to a training ship is not a wise choice either!

Before making off any breast-ropes, enquire what time that boat is leaving in the morning. They all tell you they must be away by 5.30 a.m. or earlier, in hopes that you will go elsewhere. For the same reason, you also tell any other would-be alongsider that a very early start is essential, it sometimes works.

Beware also, of inadvertently trying to force a berth between the twin hulls of a catamaran, once observed being attempted by a senior member of our school on a foggy night in Yarmouth, It does no good to the *gelcoat* or one's esteem, as the rest of your fleet will quickly hear of any such incident and make sure that you never live it down.

6. Tidal Calculations

You may not often have the privilege of giving some sailing experience to a handicapped young person, but their courage and trust is a joy. After being carried fireman fashion, across the obstacles of four other boats when rafted up fifth one out at Lymington town quay, John was asked if he had been frightened during his undignified transportation to the pontoon. His reply was "I was bloody terrified, but it was worth every minute!" The wheelchair followed with comparative ease.

To save having to repeat his ordeal in Yarmouth, permission was gained from the harbourmaster to tie up against the wall. "You will have just two hours of depth there!" he reminded us.

This time, John was easily winched across to the quayside on the end of the boom, and off we all went down the well-worn path to join the other elbow benders at the group-therapy class in *The Bugle*.

Barely an hour had passed before being excitedly hailed by Dennis, another of the skippers, "Which do you want first, the good news or the bad news?" Before having time to decide, he related "The good news is that we've had a cracking sail to the Needles and back while you lot are idling in here, and the bad news is that you are aground! — but don't worry, I've tied you to a lamp post!"

"That's impossible! The harbourmaster said 2:30 p.m., and it's only just after one o'clock, pull the other one!" Entrusting the landlord with abandoned drinks, we hastened to go and look, to find that it certainly was possible, sitting in the mud at a crazy angle, and of moderate interest to the ferry passengers.

Our lucky Cornish Pixie in Mevagissy harbour
"... look up chart datum, someone!"

May 1980

44

It took half an hour to find the harbourmaster and winkle him out from his hiding place. He was almost on his knees with apologies, I thought he was going to cry, it's not often you see officials grovel "I had forgotten that the clocks went back last night!" he whimpered.

Nothing left to do now but go back, finish the drinks, have another, and resolve to look up our own tide-tables next time.

A quiet river, such as Beaulieu, can still cause little problems to the unwary if the tidal range is not considered before trying to reach *The Master Builder's* in time for lunch. One remiss Frenchman naively overlooked a marker and cut the corner. It was hard to say how long he had been there, but we came upon him when rounding the bend. He was desperately shouting and flailing his arms, as they do, his boat, anchored, was just beginning to suggest an impish angle, and it wasn't bobbing about much either!

Repressing the first instincts to laugh and swish past, our better natures came to the fore, as there was also a young family on board, well, *Entente Cordiale* and all that, even if we don't like their *Golden Delicious*!

Our skipper decided that it would be a very good exercise for us to stop and help. Lengthy instructions in *Franglais* and miming eventually got his kedge anchor up and him rowing across with a tow-rope, with which, in a cloud of black smoke he was successfully dragged off the mud. Meanwhile, *Madame* was trying to manoeuvre their boat in an attempt to reach him, but although rowing frantically against the fast ebbing tide, he was rapidly disappearing back into the Solent with a look of Gallic disbelief on his face.

"Yes?" — "No, we can't leave him like that!" So, while still in 'Boy Scout' mode, it was agreed political to go to fetch him back as *les enfants* were looking a bit worried and we still had his tow-rope, anyway. Towing his dinghy at five knots against a two knot ebb gave him a very interesting ride and us a slight smirk. I don't think he saw the funny side, especially when he was handed three feet of frayed, knotted warp that some wag found in the locker, instead of his own coil of rope. It took a little time to dawn that the English do have a very strange sense of humour, then invited us all for a drink aboard his boat that evening. Strange that we never found where he had moored!

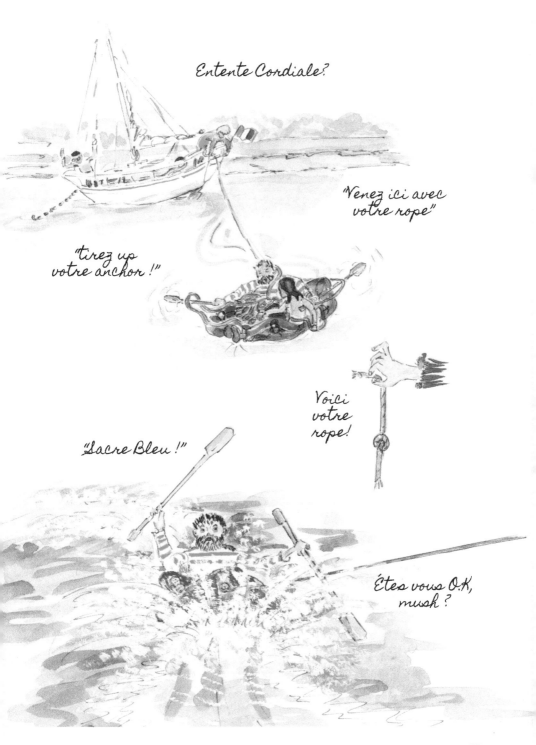

A Corner of Yarmouth Harbour

M. Matterson.

When mooring up to a buoy in a river, it helps to know the cross-section of the channel.

Wivenhoe is a delightful Essex village, almost untouched by time, up the river Colne. The first time we found it, the tide had begun to ebb and the depth was going down rapidly as we scanned for a suitable slot to moor in. On the bank almost next to the Rose and Crown, sat three *Last of the summer wine* characters enjoying the last of their wild boar pate sandwiches and beer. Jumping up, they shouted for us to throw our warps and they would pull the boat into "this 'ere" mud berth that was assuredly available.

No problem, this was *Cirdan* the bilge-keeler, and it was so lucky to be right in the village, in time for lunch, and only eight yards from the pub! The three sun-wizened garden gnomes waved goodbye and scuttled off laughing — as well they might, for, twenty minutes later there was this lop-sided sensation and all the mugs slid onto the floor. When the mast had been safely tied to the *Rose and Crown* flag-pole, it seemed appropriate to patronise it.

"Is yours the boat that has fallen over?" was the greeting from behind the bar, in front of the bar, and nearly every table.

Lunch for five was prepared with difficulty; tomatoes do not stay on the plates at a 35 degree angle.

A train ride to Colchester made an interesting diversion whilst whiling away the time waiting for the water to come back, and also helped to avoid the smirking viewers.

Mud-berths are perfectly adequate providing your boat is centrally cradled in the hollow, but half-way along the sides is not!

Tidal Miscalculations

The next trip to Wivenhoe shortly after was made with Sam's prim, fastidious sister, her husband and a determination not to get caught again by those wily locals.

This time we would be independent and pick up a buoy opposite and then use the dinghy — that should give the guests something to play at.

All went well until sometime before dawn when there came a wailing noise, a shriek and a succession of heavy thuds that permeated our slumber. Sister Irene, being on the port side, had been shovelled out of her bunk and was lying in a most undignified heap, unable to climb back in nor see the funny side of her dislodgement. Our aft-cabin too, showed signs of tilt!

Dawn revealed the many varieties of wading birds, geese, and gulls fighting and foraging for their breakfast in the deep 'V' cleft of the muddy river bed.

Marooned and surrounded by unctuous mud for four hours did not fire our visitors with enthusiasm for more after their first introduction to sailing.

7. Recovery of a man overboard

This exercise is also important for rescuing a can of beer, a packet of cigarettes or the woolly pom-pom hat that Aunty Doris knitted especially for this week. The dreaded 'man' overboard procedure is usually practised using a precious fender and goes something like this:-

You are just beginning to enjoy having been allowed to take the helm and can now keep up to wind with a glass in one hand, when the skipper furtively sneaks past and tries to slide out the best fender from the cockpit locker, hide it behind his back, whistling and trying to look casual.

Recovering 'man' overboard

"What happened?"

53

You will then be nudged or kicked by another crew member who had the same experience yesterday, giving you a few seconds to assemble your wits before the 'man' is flung astern and Skipper shouts "Man overboard!"

Instantly you have forgotten everyone's name and which instruction to give first — "Ease the boathook! You, point to the mainsheet! Oi, wots yer name, slacken the man. Ready about, hold my beer, — oh heck!"

The chap you instructed to keep pointing to the 'man' is confused, he has lost him between the waves, sails, and eager helpers during the erratic manoeuvres, but if we don't retrieve 'him', we will all have to pay for a replacement, hence the same urgency as the real thing.

Meanwhile, skipper is timing you with his saucer-sized chronometer. Three crew are jostling for the boathook as each one tries to capture and wind on the three feet of warp — a kind skipper will thoughtfully make a loop in it, so saving on the number of times it drops off.

When, at last, recovery is complete, your 'man' could be pronounced dead through hypothermia, then you do not get a tick in your log-book.

I did not consider it was fair play when one skipper threw out the 'man' when I was on a run, goose-winged with a preventer, at two knots, while the crew were sun-bathing on the fore-deck, just so that he could draw attention to my limitations!

Man or woman overboard can happen most unexpectedly to the newcomer with bi-focals particularly when stepping into the dinghy from the boat or a pontoon; so, wearers beware, and make quite sure that one foot has located the dinghy before launching off with the other one.

One lady was very lucky, or unlucky, depending on which view is taken. She stepped off and plunged, both feet together, between pontoon and dinghy, down to the bottom of the harbour and shot straight up again like a cork. Still staring directly ahead, arms by sides, she was grabbed by the shoulders, hauled up and plonked into a bemused sitting position back on the pontoon still clutching her handbag. Completely unfazed, "What happened?" she asked!

8. Pilotage

Definition:- The art of conducting a boat in and out of harbours, or along the coast i.e. finding your way visually.

Some of this can be done with the help of an AA road map or leaflet picked up from the tourist information centres, but to invest in a good up-to-date chart and pilot book has its advantages, as you will be able to confuse the helmsman with interesting instructions. "When the gap in the hedge is in transit with the left-hand edge of a black cowshed, alter course to 010 degrees until a skull-shaped rock bears 270 degrees, then aim for the single tall tree until the *Crown and Anchor and Jolly Sailor* appear to converge, you should see the moorings then."

Usually, the ensuing arguments wake up the ones trying to feign sleep, who then participate with their views, by which time you are probably on the sand-bar.

In unfamiliar waters the name of a buoy is always on the other side. On sailing up closer to look, you will find that the gulls and cormorants have been busy whitewashing it and by now the tide is sweeping you well past so that buoy no longer matters and interest turns to the next one.

"See that smoke over there on the cliffs? That is the

rubbish tip, and if you point between the headland and the smoke you'll just about miss the rocks on the corner. Then when you think you are going straight into that different coloured strip of cliffs, turn left — I think."

When coming into Poole at night, once past the chain ferry, the guy or gal with the least experience will feel very chuffed to be given the helm and told to follow the buoys up to the town quay. The rest of the crew then hand out cans of beer to all but you then wander off.

Three casually loll on the bow swapping jokes; the others are below easing off their boots and bladders. All around you are flashing lights, multitudes of them, like technicoloured glow-worms. Brain adjusts to sorting out the car rear lights from the traffic lights and helps you find some port and starboard ones in between but, WHERE is the next flashing red?

Shouting for help from your colleagues only gets the same response "Keep going, stay between the reds and greens, anyone want anoth—" Thud!! Well, how was I to know there was an unlit red buoy on a bend? Not my fault!

Having narrowly missed being catapulted over the bow, the three return, slightly shaken, vowing they had honestly been keeping a good lookout. Skipper "tut- tuts" inferring that nobody can be trusted with anything, as he performed the mud-shuffle off the bank to the moans, curses and blame-shifting as we were now too late for last orders at *The Helmsman*.

So, forget about it being a privilege to be offered the helm when coming into port, just be polite and say "No thank you, you take it," to some other eager Competent Crewman!

Navigation

M. M.

"What rock?"

Poole Harbour
June 1977.

Identification of lights and buoys.
— And the unlit ones

Rustic charm of the South-East coast

'Dee-Lea'

High Tech !

'Cirdan'
on her mud berth,
Maldon Essex

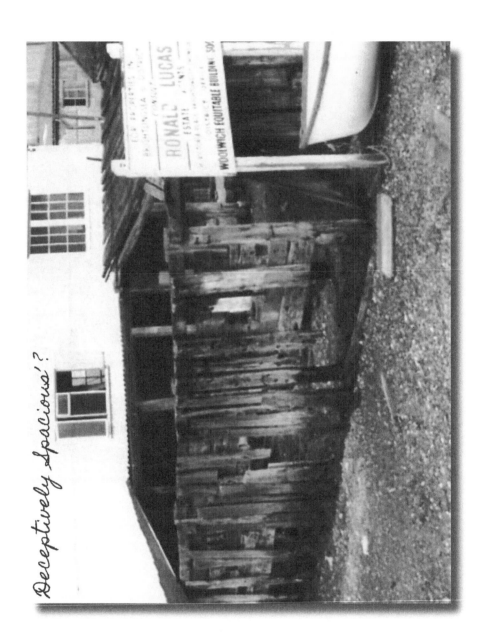

Deceptively Spacious'?

Low water!
Mersea

Chapter Six

Bog-hopping and Withy-baiting in Backwaters

After a few terms experiencing these revelations and passing the preliminary practical examinations, we were considered to be sufficiently competent to take even less competent aspiring sailors out for weekend 'jollies' in order to attain their necessary sea miles and night hours.

The requirements then, in 1978, before being eligible to take the Yachtmaster's exam were:-

- 20 days on a cruising yacht as an active crewmember.
- 500 miles logged in tidal waters.
- 12 hours at sea by night, i.e. between sunset and sunrise.

The fact that we had a boat and not too many others at the school were lucky enough, there followed many interesting weekends spent with a wide variety of characters from all walks of life and age groups, trying to clock-up a few extra miles more than their mates.

To make access slightly easier, *Cirdan* was moved from Burnham-on-Crouch over to a mud-berth in Maldon thus being able to step on board at any time, though not necessarily meaning that you could go anywhere.

The water sneaked up and arrived about one and a half hours before high water, then disappeared with amazing rapidity shortly afterwards, so if you were not quick enough off the mark to get the timing right, you were a long time in the centre trickle studying the habits of the ducks.

It always seemed to be mid-winter when our four allocated crew would arrive with their gardening wellies, multi-coloured woolly hats, a bag of bottles, and little else but overwhelming enthusiasm and "Where's the Chippie?"

Having appeased their appetite for food, they were now craving for instant adventure. Anxious to appear seamanlike, the one with the green pom-pom enquired "Mr Skipper, *Sah*, what time is our E.T.A?" Surely not tonight, I thought, it's bedtime!

That is how we came to be torchlight withy-hunting on an extremely crisp December night, just because high water happened to be at 11:30 p.m. and no-one but us wanted to wait until mid-day.

Once past the town, there was complete darkness and the only one or two buoys were insignificant and unlit, as if no-one was expected to foolishly venture out at night from these backwaters.

The narrow winding river had no other features but reeds and withies pointing their eerie, frost-rimed fingers into the black sky. A withy has been defined as a "drunken tree so placed as to lead you aground". This is a very astute observation, as Cirdan unsettled the mud on every bend, whilst the lads tried to seek them out in the torch-beams and notice whether it was one with a green strip of farmer's plastic cow-cake bag or red binder twine.

It was so cold that the mist froze into white crusts on eyebrows and beards, startling the gulls and ducks into a frenzy at their disturbed sleep.

It took three hours of slodge and grope to thankfully reach Bradwell Marina. Going aground again at the entrance is just part of the routine. "That's another eight miles and THREE night hours chaps, wasn't it fun?"

The keen frost of the previous night did not give forth the expected bright sunny morning. Through the grey mist of fine drizzle the green pom-pom was sighted rowing back with wild flourish, bearing gifts. "Creep!" muttered someone.

"Good morning Mr Skipper, *Sah*, where is our intended destination today?", "Do we really have to go anywhere?" were my sentiments.

"Sorry Nigel, but rowing across to fetch the bread and papers does not count as sea-miles either, just a kind gesture!"

"But I took the rubbish as well, Sah!"

Spending the whole day getting thoroughly soaked in featureless surroundings, just sailing nowhere in particular is not to everyone's taste, but these five young men were enjoying every minute, reminding me of the sailor's proverb which says:-

> *He that would go to sea for pleasure*
> *would go to hell for a pastime!*

The rain increased from a steady downpour to monsoon proportion as they tied up with only thoughts of fish'n'chips and bright lights.

It was a bit late and Brightlingsea was closed. There was not a chip-shop, café or pub serving food to be seen as we trudged gloomily through the puddles in the dark streets "I'm si-iinging in the rain, just si-ii— "

"Shut Up! Who's great idea was this, then? I'd like to knock his pom-pom off!" Sagging spirits soared when a lighted window came into view, it was a Chinese Restaurant, a bit smarter than befitted this bedraggled crew, but if they would serve us food, that was all that mattered.

The door opened with startling clang, letting in a furious gust of wet air to set their oriental wind chimes into a frenzy, and diverting the interest of a score of well-heeled diners from their Chicken Chow-Mein.

Seven bedraggled beings dripped and squelched across to the reception desk, parked the current rubbish bag in the corner, and politely enquired about the possibility of a table from the two bow-tied inscrutables. They were remarkably civil, considering all the water dripping on their floor, but were obviously glad of the chance of extra trade on such a foul night.

"Yes, yes, we have table, You been climbing mountains?" There seemed no answer to that!

"You must go up to Waldringfield." Advised a friendly local, "Moor off *The Maybush*, and go to see the large originals of Giles' cartoons on the walls of the bar. It's a tricky little entrance to the river Deben, the tide runs about four knots on the ebb, and you only have enough depth at the entrance for one and a half hours either side of high water. When you think you are heading straight for the beach, turn sharply to starboard by the black can — if you see it!"

Such instructions are usually enough to put us right off a place, but the attraction of the cartoons and *The Maybush* overcame the apprehension.

The Pier and Big Wheel at Clacton-on-sea were easily recognised, as was Frinton-on-sea and Walton-on-the-Naze

"You been climbing mountains?"
—Brightlingsea 1978

and then came a vast expanse of nothing across Pennyhole Bay.

A large ferry identified Harwich in time to avert a "bit of a domestic", so this must be Felixstowe next. "Can't be far now." Binoculars scour the beach-line for clues. "I can see a building, there is writing on it, just a minute, I think there is a 'D', and perhaps an 'L' yes, it's the Ladies Toilet next to an ice-cream stall. I think we are a bit too close in, there's a man swimming towards us, oh, guess what, it's that little black buoy!"

Apart from a slight tide-rip, the entrance gave no problem, so why all the warnings? The river Deben is tranquil and pastoral, with the cows from the meadows meandering down to drink, and luck gave us a convenient buoy right outside *The Maybush*.

Since etiquette dictates that you should not enter a bar just to look at the pictures on the walls, adequate time for full appreciation was allotted to the evening pilgrimage so that all details and local brew could be absorbed with pleasure.

High water next day was at a sociable hour, so a peaceful undisturbed night passed. I can't remember who rose first to make this disconcerting revelation, "The pub's gone!"

It was there last night, was it a dream? Surely not, I have a headache to prove that I went somewhere! When the eyes and brain kicked into gear, we could accept that it certainly was not where we had left it! Had someone moved the boat for a joke? The warps were secure; it was the same buoy, so where had *The Maybush* gone to?

Thoughts turned to more currently important matters, such as breakfast and how many eggs do you want, poached,

River Deben, Suffolk

Matterson
1979

boiled or fried? "Another cup of tea? There's plenty of time — what was that?" I asked. "What was what?" — muffled thud, then again a few seconds later.

Up on deck, there hiding behind a clump of trees, a hundred yards up river, appeared the lost pub! The situation slowly dawned — we were dragging a bucket-full of cement on the end of a balloon, termed as a mooring.

It was only a hint of a slight jerking sensation, followed by a barely discernible thud, back up-river, having dragged it down on last night's ebb! Half an hour later we seemed to be jogging along nicely, rearranging the visitors' moorings. There were not many options open, as there was not yet enough depth at the entrance, but, not wishing to take the River Authority's bucket of concrete to sea with us, chose to cast it free in a useful position and try to look casual.

An approaching power-boat seemed a promising chance, so, swallowing pride, we smiled, waved and quickly fell in right behind it, if he can get out now, I'm sure a bilge-keel boat can; with a bit of luck!

Keeping as close as expedient in the wake of the power-boat, the angry little chop was nicely ironed out flat, the echo-sounder bleeped unheeded until the vicious ebb spat it's vessels into the open water, where we felt it would be politic to acknowledge our leader with another wave.

It was then that this little note was found on the chart, printed in red ink:-

Woodbridge Haven - The bar on the
river Deben varies in position and depth.
The buoys and leading beacons are moved
to conform with changes in the channel.

Entrance should not be attempted
without local knowledge!

Ready now to try more new ground, or a different shade of mud, perhaps Walton Backwaters might be interesting? "There is the beach, lots to do and we could have an ice-cream!" wheedled the family.

I think it was called Foundry Creek or some similar picturesque name where the water petered out, leaving panoramic views of steep mud-banks, wrecks, and drunken beacons which had long since lost their purpose, topped off with a strip of grass somewhere level with the top of the mast.

With thoughts that it might look better at high water, Cirdan retraced a short distance back to the row of moorings to find a buoy. Wiser now, we chose the largest one available, then set off for the rest of the way up to Walton-on-the-Naze in the dinghy and left it on a rickety pontoon, a few planks missing, but the only one we could see.

An afternoon at this typical family seaside town made a welcome change from tides and mud, as we became children again with the throng on the beach.

"I told you there wasn't time for another ice-cream!" whinged number one son as he plothered twenty yards back to the water, dragging the dinghy over the sloppy black goo with his girlfriend sitting in it because she refused to have "that stuff" oozing up between her toes and round the knees!

Chapter Seven

Up the ladder

Each year, the New Parks Community Centre organised reserved carriages on the train for the London Boat Show, and a bus for the Southampton one. Both were well attended as the cost was extremely modest. It was at the 1979 Show in Southampton after dallying at the Guinness stand in the warm sunshine, that we became drawn to a tough-looking ketch built in Finland.

It was still only 32 feet long, but it looked big to us, and had the first walkthrough aft cabin we had seen, at that time, in a boat of that size. Having spent two years of undoing hatches to cross over the cockpit, undo the main saloon hatches to get to the heads on a cold or wet night, this cosy double aft cabin seemed a very attractive feature, as did the teak decks, and it would certainly be a step up the ladder from *Cirdan*.

After a subtle intimation that this boat could now be classed as a 'demonstration' model, there came an offer of an equally attractive price, plus the opportunity to change our sailing ground for one with slightly less mud. We decided to go for it that very afternoon before bravado wore off and common sense intervened.

Choosing a name was not easy. At first, we tried to find a bird's name in Finnish, but the spellings were far too unwieldy or unpronounceable. A book from the library on

Going ashore in Bray, Isle of Alderney

Finnish folklore gave us *Kalevala*, Land of heroes and since Cirdan was a literary boat-builder, we were looking for a parallel, but the one in this epic tale had a name far too long and clumsy to be battled with on the radio. So, we settled for Kalevala.

After the extravagance of the new boat, a wave of thrift, (or tightfistedness) motivated the making of our own 'dodgers', a family game played on the kitchen floor with forty four white strips, two blue backgrounds, and lashings of glue. The results were quite impressive after the mess was cleaned up.

A week or so later, when filling in the forms for the Lloyd's registry, we thought to just check the name again, "Oh ---- ! You know those six little white bits we found under the table and thought were scrap? They were the legs off the 'E' !" Too late now, so that is how our Marina 95 came to be called *Kalivala* instead of *Kalevala*, of the Finnish folklore.

Up the ladder too, with our R.Y.A. course-work at evening classes and practical assessments too, being made much easier now having a mooring on the river Hamble.

Easter week and the Spring Bank holiday week were the highlights of the New Parks sailing fraternity, when you passed or failed your practical exams. Between 15 and 20 boats would be issued with up to seven assorted aspiring, over-eager crew, to be moulded into some sort of sailor by their long-suffering skippers within the next week.

During those weeks, Sam had begun to assess a few students for 'Competent crew' or Coastal 1. with the help of a couple more experienced ones needing sea-miles, and I was dispatched to another boat to prevent me from "sticking my oar in" and arguing with Sam.

It was expected that each boat would submit a log book of their passages to be judged for the coveted prize, an impressive silver cup that was out of all proportion to the log itself and I was coerced into writing one.

Not being too well versed with the technical bits, I tended to pad it out with a hint of nonsense and pictures to make sound more interesting. That is why I have these sketches lying about all these years later!

The first seat of learning in this practical training week is a stool in the Square Rigger. Under the heading of 'Passage Planning', each Skipper is making exaggerated predictions of ambitious trips to Cherbourg and the Channel Islands — weather permitting — whilst at the same time weighing up the chances of realising these plans with the unlikely looking crew he's been allocated.

Optimism is fired anew by the view through the bottom of each upturned glass.

On arriving at your given boat, it is prudent to let your status be known. Usually, two ladies will share the large double aft cabin regardless of whether they are with their husbands. It did happen that a young couple arrived on board together and were thoughtfully given a rather small fore-peak cabin. It was not until almost the end of the week that the lady revealed that she had only accepted a lift down from Leicestershire with the chap, but otherwise had never met him before and had not liked to say anything! She didn't know him - but she does now!

Safety.

1. Life jackets.

One of the first things to learn will be how to put on your life jackets and harnesses and, most importantly, remember where to find them. Usually, they will be hidden under the Skipper's bunk along with the crates of U.H.T. milk and bread, so it is diplomatic to try not to need these items while he is off-watch — unless you really intend to annoy him.

Harnesses come in an interesting array of straps and buckles so designed as to lead to confusion on the first encounter. We came across one type, half red, half blue, all apparently in one piece with no obvious method of getting into it.

It took seven adults and a young lad half an hour of contortions and undignified variations on the approved method, which were hindered by unrepeatable suggestions. The boy was the first to solve it, proving that concerted effort and perseverance eventually succeeds, and now most members can don their harnesses providing there is no immediate emergency. Our plumbing engineer still favoured the 'Y Front' method.

2. The Life Raft.

Hopefully, not being an experience that one often has the chance to find out *for real*, leaves you wondering what it would really be like to have to cope with a life-raft in an emergency.

Our Sailing School managed to book the Public Baths in Leicester for one night, so that those who wished could find out without too much drama.

Having a great fear of my face being under water in any circumstances, I panic for air, so I thought that this might be a worthwhile experience and could even be fun too.

An assembly of life-jacketed, plimsolled enthusiasts in ancient and ragged oilskins noisily sorted themselves into groups of six, many of whom I did not know.

The Life-raft was inflated at the deep end and the first six took the plunge amidst shouts of encouragement. Then it was our turn. Being thrown out of the raft was not too traumatic, although it was hard work trying to manoeuvre in oilskins. I did not mind being trapped underneath when the raft turned over, it was having to take that deep breath and dive out from under it that I dreaded most of all.

Eyes tightly closed, gasping, I spluttered to the surface to grab a hand-hold, we counted heads as instructed - all correct - so now came the struggle to turn the monster the right way up. It is not easy, just as you think it's nearly over, it slips out of grasp and you start again.

The one with the most breath left finds he has volunteered to get back in first and is pushed, or impeded, from behind as he drags himself up and back inside to help the next man in. There are no courtesies now, grab each survivor by the seat of the trousers or any other grabbable part and dump them in a water-logged heap as quickly as possible to safely.

"Right, that's the lot, better have another count just to check. One, two, three, four, five,— there's someone missing, count again!" We call out our names; raise our hands in turn, still only five. "We've lost somebody, keep quiet, start again, this could happen in a real emergency, one, two,—"

There came an almost inaudible gasp and a whispery voice said, "It's me, John, you're all sitting on me, and I'm not very big!"

3. Use of flares.

Class night on Bonfire Night gives everyone the opportunity to hold, set off, and see the effects of most types of flares without calling the attention of the Lifeboat or the local Constabulary. It also gives the skippers a great opportunity to dispose of their obsolete flares without too much conscience, since it can be classed as Further Education!

4. Shoes

It is safer to wear shoes on deck when sailing. This prevents toe injuries caused by aggressive cleats, tracks, and misplaced objects, and also guards against hurtful words from fellow crew when they trip over them in the saloon. At night keep them at hand to hurl at the ones who snore at both ends simultaneously.

5. The importance of warm clothing.

When the body starts to feel cold, the brain will begin to lose interest in the job in hand and no longer cares what the top-mark is on yonder buoy. Then nausea creeps in. To dress in several warm layers, including unisex thermals is recommended but not necessarily enjoyed by the fashion-conscious.

One of the problems is judging sufficient time to get to the heads. Ladies must count the layers pulled down, and check the same number up again. Missing one out in either direction can cause discomfort, embarrassment, or just trip you up.

Hypothermia creeps up insidiously. A person becomes very quiet, glazed, vacant, and unwilling to move, which, in some crew is quite their normal state, making it more difficult to notice, especially the one 'hugging a bucket'.

It is said that it can be treated by enveloping the patient in foil, like an oven-ready turkey, or the proximity of another body in a sleeping-bag.

Although I have never had cause to test these theories, the practicalities of both methods in full foul-weather gear make it sound preferable to keep your inside warm with frequent hot drinks and food - see *Down the hatch*.

Sea-sickness tablets can cause drowsiness at inconvenient times.

Safety - Fitting the harness

Concerted effort and perseverence!

Lifeboat Drill

"... one, two, three, four, five ... where's six ?"

Some tablets can cause drowsiness at inconvenient times...

6. Use of dinghy.

When you have watched a rival boat deftly row out his lines to the trots, you might think "I can do that—easy!" So try to earn a few Brownie Points by offering to row out with the stern warp.

A coil of rope can tie itself into knots even as it lies quietly at rest in the bottom of the dinghy. Perhaps there is no need to row, as you are swept by the tide into the cat's cradle of lines which prompt one oar to leap overboard. Reach for it and risk being garrotted on a seaweed draped, slimy warp from another decade.

After ducking and dodging through to the ring and passing your line through it, you are now ready to proudly return to the chap waiting on the stern with a drink in his hand. No-one has told you yet how easy it is to pull yourself hand-over-hand along the other trot-lines back to the boat! So there you are, rowing against the tide with the line between your teeth, and trying not to ensnare the oars.

The once-patient chap on the stern is now getting peevish, he's finished his beer, the others have gone below and he's getting cold. Twenty minutes later you are still trying to reach your boat. For some reason unknown, you keep catapulting back to the trot-pile; your composure has melted into a frustration just short of screaming.

This simple operation has now become a spectator sport with bets being taken and added shouts of encouragement adding to your acute embarrassment. But what they didn't know was that just below the surface of the water was an unseen lurking warp which had hooked itself round the black rubber painter knob just under the bow of the dinghy, shooting it back to the pile like an arrow from a bow!

So if you do volunteer, it is as well to be aware of these little trials that can damage your pride.

Moorng up on trots, with use of a dinghy

It can be dangerous to overload your dinghy !

Chapter Eight

On the Wall

1. Weather.

*"There are warnings of gales in all areas. New low,
995 centred over Wight, Portland and Plymouth..."*

Modern technology now gives regular updated read-outs of
all weather systems, but it was not always so. On a week of
practical training, you will be required to take a little more
in-depth interest than holding up a wet finger or consulting
the seaweed.

The R.Y.A. insisted that students must learn to take
down weather reports from the radio and transcribe it onto
a chart. Rotas were drawn up so that you knew when you
were cooking, navigating, checking the engine, (Ladies note
- the dipstick is always on the furthest side and makes a very
uncomfortable reach across the cylinder head!), or taking
down the weather.

There is a pecking order, the greener you are, the more
unsociable is the time for your forecast. If it is your first
trip, expect to be invited to take down the midnight or 6
a.m. forecast, when you can hear the music of *Sailing by*
between the barracking "There are some of us wanting to
sleep, you know!" If you are eager to tot up more sea-miles,
then you listen in hopes of a good sail tomorrow; if not,

you wish the wind to be too strong, enabling you to go and buy that gadget you saw yesterday, a new set of waterproofs and wellies perhaps, or that 36" wooden ship's wheel which proved to be irresistible at the price.

With space on board being already limited, you may not be too popular when looking for a place to put it, but there should be at least one helpful person who will readily advise you! Being storm-bound can be very boring when festering with six or seven other damp bodies. Suffering yet another of skippers edifying quizzes in a leaky saloon, an alternative is a culture tour of the town's surrounding back streets. They can throw up some interesting discoveries without having to resort to the pub or the shops yet again!

Whilst trying to find a refuge from the current deluge at Dartmouth, we saw a soggy notice flapping from a telegraph pole, an arrow pointing to "Third-hand books", which seemed like a promising respite from the rain. Three more signs and two flights of steps later, there was St Barnabus' Church with more steps up to a doorway festooned with Christmas decorations, Fairy Lights and feather dusters. The mildewed interior was obviously no longer a church, yet the hymn-boards remained with their numbers askew. The chipped plaster Madonna looked down in forlorn disbelief at the conglomeration of humanity's domestic chuck-outs, where the petals of her long-dead flowers had fallen.

Battered boxes of 'house clearance' clutter piled high amongst the bookcases, each, no doubt, with its own sad story. From the vestry came the sound of an electric saw and the mixed smells of linseed oil, shellac, and spirit being used by two men busy restoring furniture.

After an hour of total absorption, we had to remind

ourselves that we were here to go sailing and must catch the next weather forecast.

A few extracts from a 1979 log narrative -

May 27

08:25 - Weather not promising, but show necessary enthusiasm by getting up for a breakfast of gargantuan proportions.

10:20 - Leave river Hamble moorings. Wind light variable. Visibility good, sea slight, intended destination Poole.

11:05 - Skipper fidgety and has the deck-hands running the Genoa up and down like a Venetian blind, saying "It's all good practise!"

12:15 - Mutiny from the crew as he shouts for the sixth sail-change just as the whisky laced with coffee is being passed up, and he admits defeat and puts the engine on.

13:55 - Wind increased, tacking through the Needles. Weather report — Night-gale imminent Wind S.W. force 6-8 expected soon.

16:50 - Very soon! Two reefs in the main and an exhilarating sail into Poole showing a well-scrubbed keel that missed the Sandbanks ferry by one and a half metres.

17:35 - Arrive into Poole harbour. Distance logged 30.9 n.miles.

It seemed that the afternoon forecast of gales had resulted in a mass convergence of an armada of small craft plus seven of our New Parks *fleet*, all jostling for a position on the town quay, milling around in a confined area, fighting a wind against tide situation whilst looking for a space. This was before the innovation of two pontoons and the latest small marina.

Mistakenly grateful, we managed to find a vacant area against the wall, made fast with all fenders out and were promptly rafted onto by five other boats in our lot who had been wise enough to let someone else get there first.

The sea was now rough in the harbour. The Harbour-master, normally a very laid-back, gentle chap, was getting harassed as he ran to and fro shouting instructions that were lost on the wind.

SHIPPING FORECAST

(1961 1500m. 200 kHz)

A ⦵ .13:55. GMT
DATE 7 . 6 . 77

GENERAL SYNOPSIS

GALES, EVERYWHERE.

FORECAST FOR SEA AREAS FOR NEXT 24 HRS

AREA	GALE	FORECAST	WIND BECOMING	WEATHER	VISIBILITY	REMARKS
			YES			
VIKING	✓			AWFUL	NIL	*!!*
FORTIES	✓			"	"	"
CROMARTY	✓			"	"	"
FORTH	✓			"	"	"
TYNE	✓			"	"	"
DOGGER	✓			"	"	"
FISHER	✓			"	"	"
GERMAN BIGHT	✓			"	"	"
HUMBER	✓			"	"	"
THAMES	✓			"	"	"

"What D'y reckon then, skip?"

REPORTS ... DEN...

GALLOPER
VARNE
ROYAL SOVEREIGN
PORTLAND BILL
SCILLY
VALENTIA
RONALDSWAY
MALIN HEAD

FAROES

VIKING

BAILEY

FAIR ISLE

HEBRIDES

ISLE STELLA

CROMARTY

FORTIES

ROCKALL

FISHER

MALIN

BELL ROCK

TYNE

DOGGER

GERMAN BIGHT

FORTH

TYNE

MALIN HEAD

TYNE

RONALDSWAY

IRISH SEA

HUMBER

DOVER

THAMES

SHANNON

LUNDY

GALLOPER

VALENTIA

FASTNET

LOW

DOVER

ROYAL SOVEREIGN

PORTLAND BILL

SORLY

PORTLAND

WIGHT

WIGHT

PLYMOUTH

SCILLY

PLYMOUTH

LOW

PORTLAND

WIGHT

SOLE

LOW

VERY LOW

FINISTERRE

BISCAY

COMMENTS — *humerous & unprintable*

HEAVY WEATHER!

A large paddle-steamer (*Waverley*) and a cargo ship were due in, there was limited space, a gale blowing, and now he had run out of planks for the wall! He was being stretched to his full official capacity.

As the waves increase, the boats begin to slam against each other, and the skippers start to take a little more interest their paintwork and strakes while prowling round the decks finding fault with the placing of the next boat's fenders. Meanwhile, two of our enterprising crew lead an assault on a few nearby building sites to look for planks to fend off fenders from the wall. The polite Policemen who stopped their car to let them cross the road, did not even raise an eyebrow.

Our evening meal of 101 meatballs, 3lbs. Peas, 9lbs, Potatoes (approx), followed by *Glensporran* lightly garnished with peaches, was suddenly interrupted by the simultaneous arrival of *Waverley* and the overdue cargo ship both making interesting manoeuvres into what appeared to be the same space! Their appropriate sound signals being completely obliterated by the whole harbour of yachts joining in with their air-horns and cheers of encouragement. Amidst the resulting chaos, it was maliciously rumoured that the harbourmaster was carried off screaming!

Most crews sought refuge from the storm in *The Helmsman* that evening, except for our two conscientious 'plank-borrowers', they spent the time, and most of the night tending warps and fenders while the rest of us pretend we never heard a sound.

The outlook on the following day was just as grim. Morale is low, Sam has 'galloping gut-rot' a disease brought back from a week in Mallorca, and complains of the wear and tear of shoe-leather, not to mention his legs, on his frequent dashes down the quayside. Joan is coughing and wheezing, Frank is seasick on these moorings, I have banged my head yet again, and Skipper is in the doldrums. Not even *Waverley* is sailing today.

A doctor from an adjacent boat examines the sick, holds a 'Well-Woman' clinic and issues prescriptions. Also prescribed is a cocktail party to boost morale. Official invitations to all New Parks boats are designed and written in the comparative calm of a telephone box, thus causing a queue.

The time was for high water Poole, which was conveniently at midday, but we are sarcastically reminded by Skipper, that we were actually on a teaching course, and not on holiday, thereupon insisting on mental exercise in the form of a nautical quiz. The resulting arguments helped to deaden the sound of the beating rain and slamming boats until party time, when thirty assorted dripping 'yotties' put the water-level interestingly near the top of the rubbing-strake. The quality of the wine passes without undue criticism as we all know that no-one will donate their good stuff, it's the quantity that counts!

It is later, and as usual, when the chef of the day is at his crucial peak of readiness, when *some-one* decides that all boats will move further down the quay — now! The verbal reaction from all crews is unprintable, but loosely suggests "Oh dearie me, what a bother." Frantic pre-occupation with the tangled mass of warps, fenders, and planks, helps to detract from the smell of burning coming from the galley and the sound of the sobbing chef.

Three boats warped together, moving down in tandem to a more favourable place causes envy and comments such as 'Clever Dick', 'Big-head', and "Well - he would, Wouldn't he?!" - Heavy weather can also be experienced next morning!

Walking the plank

The Commodore's cocktail party - H.W. Poole May 28th 1979

2. Basic knowledge of engines.

When first learning to manoeuvre under power, it is an advantage to know how to start and stop, remembering that a yacht has no brakes. If you sense that the pontoon is hurtling towards you unexpectedly, you can try a sharp reverse thrust panic, and you will then also learn that most boats have a devious reaction in reverse gear and may respond completely opposite to your intentions. At this stage, do not let the shouting fluster you, you can hand the wheel or tiller smartly back to the skipper or just wait for the crunch!

Students should acquaint themselves with the positions of the water and fuel intakes and not wait until after a nozzle has been removed before thinking to read the wording on the filler-cap.

Each crew member is usually allocated a day or time to be on engine duty i.e. he, or she is responsible for checking the alternator belt, engine hours, and levels of fuel and oil.

Ladies in particular will note that the accessibility of the dipstick is directly adverse to the height, girth, and comfort of the operator!

3. Simple maintenance.

It is always a comfort to know that you have an enthusiastic engineer on board who can cheerfully deal with blocked sinks or heads without nausea or grizzling, as one reluctant volunteer did, "you can't expect a three inch diameter *log* to pass through a two inch hole whoever it was!"

Our gem was usually to be found attempting the impossible on his knees, wreathed in tobacco smoke from his obnoxious pipe. It was in our own interests not to complain, "Facing Mecca?" someone asked through the haze. Not so, he's just upset that the cruise is nearly over and feels the urge to disembowel the sewage system yet again before returning to port!

If the carpet floats when the sea is calm and it's not raining into the open hatch, the fault may be traced back to the "eager beaver" who washed up last. If he denies all knowledge of it, then you can spend an interesting hour taking up the saloon floorboards to search for a disconnected waste-pipe whilst the rest of the crew grumble in the cockpit.

Maintenance - Basic knowledge of engines

Our team of engineers

Chapter Nine

Down the Hatch

This chapter heading, has perhaps been used many times before, but it still seems appropriate.

Victualing.

> *"For the well-being of the body and morale, a well-balanced diet is essential. Badly planned meals can lead to abnormal bowel conditions."*

By partially ignoring this wisdom, it is possible to provision your boat for a week at sea without too many complaints. It is not easy to cater for all tastes, as each prospective crew member has their own preferences and you have only met them for one hour, the week previously.

Ignore the one who claims to be partial to fresh trout with almonds, can only drink fresh ground coffee or must have squeezed ripe oranges for breakfast "—if that's alright with you!" Keep it simple. Porridge is excellent comfort fodder, hot, nourishing, and tastes the same coming up as it did going down.

Our school also held the belief that, in order to maintain ones strength and allay sea-sickness, you should have something sustaining every half an hour, even if the crossing was only from Lymington to Yarmouth. It then became tradition that each person brought down a good solid rib-sticking fruit cake with the other items on their list, yielding 51.42 degrees per person per day and so heavy as to be virtually non-returnable, although the hyper-sensitive stomachs may prove otherwise.

As much fresh food as possible is taken, so do not complain if you find yourself having to share an aft cabin, not only with a stranger, but also with a sack of potatoes, a bag of onions, box of cauliflowers, and a stone of carrots. The smell is not too bad at first, it's towards the end of the week when you begin to wonder "who it is, or what it is and where it is?" A navigator, in a moment of stress, was heard to mutter that "We have more breeding cauliflowers than bloody charts." he just needed a bit of humouring before being entrusted with the duty of cutting the cake. He was the one with the dividers.

Good relationships are not fostered by stowing the thirty boxes of U.H.T. milk under the bunks, but they've got to go somewhere, how are you to know where the skipper is choosing to sleep?!

By the time everything is stowed, the water-line will be well down on the norm, but those three whole cheeses, the crates of ale, wine, and seven bottles of whisky were all essentials, "did anyone remember the toilet rolls?"

Crisps and nibbles do not keep their ultimate freshness when stored in the heads, even in a plastic bag, but any surplus past its best can be used for barter or taken as a generous gesture when visiting other boats.

Tins of vegetables, beef stew, and new potatoes, are a good stand-by on or after a long passage. Even the most galley-shy member can tip 3 tins (A+B+C) into a large pan, heat, and serve in bowls with a spoon as 'Dog's Dinner' or

Lady crewmember working for Costal ~~SS~~
- Expurgated version !

"Activities in the galley can lead to burns, cuts
and asphyxia..."

'Cut-and-come-again soup'.

Whether you are aspiring to pass your test for Competent Crew, Day Skipper, or Yachtmaster, you will be expected to produce at least one breakfast, lunch, and evening meal, so it is well to come prepared with a simple, rehearsed recipe, and not say "I wouldn't know how to make a Spaghetti Bolognese even if it was tinned!" and that was the wife of a budding Day Skipper who had volunteered to cook supper on her husband's behalf.

At the other extreme are the ones who are obviously trying very hard to impress their seniors with sumptuous meals, and regular dainty morsels which were secretly hidden on board, not on the stores list, but certainly intended to win acclaim.

It became a popular challenge, especially for inter-boat bragging, to make your own bread whilst on passage. This homely occupation seemed to make the current helmsman and navigator a little peevish when being frequently asked to "please change tack to get the sun back onto the rising dough." Liquid bribery often had to be resorted to until a successful rising was agreed and we could be re-orientated back on course.

One skipper's attempt produced a batch of rock-hard brown lumps intended to be wholemeal rolls, "I must have killed the yeast when I put them under the grill to rise!" was the excuse. During the peacefulness of his afternoon nap, I regret to say, that the rest of the crew had their sport by sending broad-side salvos of the offending rolls across to the basking sharks off Mevagissy.

When you are beating, bucking crazily, and the horizon,

when visible, is on 'tilt', someone will start craving for sustenance. Often it is the helmsman, who wants to make sure that no-one is going to relieve him while he's having fun. "How about some soup then?"

If you fail to look vitally occupied at this moment, then it will be your lot to go down and make it, unless you feign instant *mal-de-mer*. Not usually afflicted, I often found I was reluctantly navigating or administering refreshment, because I could tolerate the conditions below deck.

Soup? Quick and foolproof! Or is it? Having catapulted down the companion-way steps, put one foot on a pencil, the other in a wayward grill pan, and skated down to the fore-peak, you can pick up the belongings of the less tidy crew whilst clawing the way back to the galley area, and rescue the chart from under the table. In doing so, the next wave puts your wet knee onto the dislodged *Reed's Almanac*, still open at the required Tide Tables, screwing up twenty pages into damp dyslexia.

Now starts the search for the soup. Everything you need will be on the windward side (Sod's Law) so, by opening the sliding cupboard you are hit in the face by a bag of rice. Deftly catching the jar of marmalade, but missing the salt pot and tea-bags, ignore the mounting disorder, and make a positive grab for the packet of soup.

The removal of the soup causes lateral displacement of other sundry condiments and the seven mugs you are going to need anyway. Cupboard door safely slammed shut, but a bit slow withdrawing fingers, feet firmly braced against the chart-table, chest on sink, you can now read that "This packet makes one gallon of soup."

A bit of mental arithmetic and adjustment to density is

"How about some soup, then?"

51.42° of fruit cake

"Water, water everywhere..."
Fetching the drop to drink

made despite the jibes of "Why are we waiting?", "What's keeping you, are you growing your own vegetables?" The kettle has boiled, you are now ready to pour.

Not to be caught out here, as the boat drops off the top of a 'big one' — line up the mugs in the sink so that they won't fall over, and there is no undue mess if you don't aim straight, it's bound to hit one mug or another. Three, four, five, six, so far so good, sev— and we drop sideways off this wave, leaving you with the sad realisation that the soup that went down the sink must not be the skipper's or the helmsman's or anyone else's — it had got to be yours!

To try and divert from disappointment and avoid pointed remarks about the condition of the *Reed's Almanac*, just try ironing its crumpled pages with a hot saucepan!

A few skippers like to prove that they are not pedantic all the time, so have a little 'party piece' for an otherwise grim evening. One had his silk dressing-gown and long cigarette holder, doing his very smooth Noel Coward bit. Another did his pancake trick, state your preference and he would toss them and bring them down on to your plate flat, or folded in half.

Of course, the occasional one stuck to the ventilator or got trodden underfoot, but this was his way of keeping up the spirits of a storm-bound crew. Any sound of hilarity from another boat would send him dashing across with his flour and tin of treacle; it was really just a ploy to get himself and his crew in on someone else's party.

Then when the judgement became befuddled, the results descended raggier and messy, missing the plates. When you had run out of eggs, they departed, leaving the washing up, and their flour and treacle, giving a good reason for returning for a repeat performance.

Beware of the ones with bagpipes, or even a recording, they do enjoy full volume on arrival and departure, in spite of an embarrassed crew.

Making a trifle on a lively beat was one of my nautical achievements, I put it in the head's washbasin for safety and it survived well, except that when I came to serve it up, it had been decorated with two awesome plastic bluebottles which had been thoughtfully bought in town by two troublemakers that morning!

Do try to remember to tell the chef of the day where you have stored current food items. "Something nasty in a basin!" Rosie screamed, as she was trying to locate her wellies in a dark corner.

"Ah, that's where we put the leftover half melon!"
Water.

This also counts as 'ship's stores', and as long as you have some, it is no problem. When the taps issue their last defiant drips when trying to make the skipper's morning tea, or halfway through the washing up when you are being hassled to "get a move on we're casting off!", then it can be a problem, and the accusations begin.

"No! Definitely not me, I wash seven mugs up in one mug of water!" The ladies usually get the blame, so if you are one of those who simply must wash her hair on board, and rinse out her undies every day, then you can expect to be muttered at.

On a good pontoon, as long as someone remembers, and you're not rafted five boats out, then filling up is easy, but if you are at anchor or in the oil-slick in the corner of a fishing harbour, then it is not always that simple.

That is how two of our stalwarts happened to be rowing against the ebb in a squall up the river Yealm with a dinghy full of plastic cans and any other available utensil.

The tide is very purposeful there, and by the time the water source was coming to view round the bend, they had run out of river, leaving an unnavigable trickle. Being resourceful, they rowed to the nearest accessible house and knocked on the back door. Fortunately, the lady of the house was sympathetic to these two dripping objects, but made them use the garden hose rather than have them in her kitchen.

"An unfelicitous business for which
I did not care one single jot."

- R.L. Stevenson

The ever popular, spacious aft cabin.
Shared not only with a stranger, but also...

Newton Ferrers - Devon. May 1980

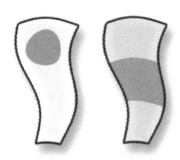

Chapter Ten

Going Foreign

Most budding yotties in the Competent Crew stage can't wait to 'cross the ditch', it all sounds so exciting and you fancy yourself as a buccaneer.

All is tranquil as you leave the river Hamble and into the Solent between Bramble Bank and Calshott Spit and not one spot of tea is spilt as you see Cowes on the port side between bites of your first 51.42 degrees of fruitcake. Yarmouth, a little way ahead, looks as welcoming as ever, but we are not going there today — we're 'Going Foreign!'

The water between Hurst Point and Fort Albert can be interestingly turbulent at times but your attention is drawn to the famous Needles ahead, pinkly glowing, innocuous in the late afternoon sun. ("*Against the snot green sea*" - James Joyce, *Ulysses*)

Once past the Bridge buoy a course may be set at thereabouts 185 degrees Compass, depending on the navigator's whim, and the Genoa sail is driving a pleasant 6 knots. That is until the wave pattern changes in the overfalls.

One by one, the crew grow quieter and by the time the Fairway buoy is astern, gastric disorientation sets in. Do not expect any sympathy. Your skipper may offer you an alternative by suggesting going back, but you don't want to provoke a mutiny at this early stage.

You also may be offered the second wedge of fruitcake

just to test your reactions.

Having now done your first two-hour watch, it is bliss to go below anticipating a welcome sleep, but you find your bunk occupied by a sail-bag and an abject human specimen hugging a bucket, so you have to find some other available space. Just remind him that,

"we are as close to heaven by sea as by land"

- Humphrey Gilbert (1537-83)

There is nothing remotely romantic about sharing the aft cabin with one of the opposite sex when dressed head to toe in thermal underwear and dripping oilskins, even if you considerately remove your wellies before slipping into someone else's warm sleeping-bag. (Hence the term 'Hot bunking'.)

Sleep is not impossible, just difficult when you bounce from every surface like a tennis ball in a box along with the other two who will now have joined you. By comparison, it is almost comfortable when the boat is heeling over well because you become stacked on the bulwarks, that is until someone on deck decides to change tack!

Just as you are drifting into a dream of warmth and comfort you are shaken back into reality and dragged out of the sleeping-bag which is then hastily occupied by an off-watch crew member.

Still in a daze, you try to absorb the boat's position and any other hasty instructions passed on in the rush for a bunk. Dawn breaks, and if you are lucky, the sun rises as you hug a mug of hot, chlorine-tainted tea and you greet the one who has now bravely let go of his bucket. "Lovely crossing, wasn't it?"

"...Yeah!!!"

There, faintly revealing itself in the morning mist, is your aim, your goal, the realisation of your first Channel crossing — CHERBOURG!! And nearly ten night hours for your log-book.

Passing through the Grande Rade there seems to be a lifting of spirits, in more than one sense, and by the time the boat is safely moored up in the marina, there is a noticeable personality change in everyone.

We are ABROAD! We must have hot croissants with apricot conserve for breakfast! The sickest ones on the crossing, who missed their night watch, make a sudden recovery and spring into action to go rushing off to find these essentials in hopes of redeeming their image.

It is also the custom to sit at a quay-side bar to practise in turn the ordering of seven beers in French. Further language lessons being taken in the evening when four boat crews converge on an unpretentious back-street bistro affectionately known as *Nora Batty's*.

This Gallic counterpart stands her ground, arms folded, awaiting decisions from her limited menu. She then writes down what she thinks you have ordered, and duly brings everyone something that she has decided you will eat, because it has all become too confusing. No-one has enough vocabulary to argue with her anyway, and it matters little after the tenth carafe of *Plonk de maison*. The arguments do begin though, when some wag suggests a night sail back after dinner!

Almudaina Arch - Palma 1981

M. Matteson

Departure

The Needles - 18:30 June 4th 1977

Return

The Needles – 14:40 June 9th 1977

Mallorca

The father of a friend of a friend of Bill, our Leicestershire Cruising Association principal, owned a 30 foot Moody called *Cap Blanco*, which was based in Palma, Mallorca. For a modest fee of £40 per person per week it could be chartered for the practical training sessions at Easter and Whitsuntide.

Although unable to pass any exams because it was not in tidal waters, it proved to be a very popular escape from the masochistic rigours of the Channel and the caprices of English weather, so you put your name down promptly.

Another £40 bought the return flight to Palma, £15 for the food and drinks kitty and £10 for meals out (1979), plus a bit extra, you could then enjoy an idle week of hedonism in calm blue waters and warm sunshine on the pretext of important education! — Or could you?

The first few hours were basically the same each time; it was the assortment of characters making up your crew that made the interesting difference to each trip. Arriving sometime after midnight, your taxi drops you off at what looks like an extensive building site. This, we are assured is the *Club Nautico Rael*, it just happens to be under refurbishment and extension — and it has been raining!

The night porter eventually rouses from slumber to let you through the gates with all the baggage and food stores you thought essential for survival in the first few hours.

A few hours of sleep and you are eager to be off sailing, but there is a slight delay. The batteries are flat, the water pumped out of the bilges has oil in, and someone has found a plastic bag containing substance of unknown origin! It was sloppy, the colour of liver, and evil-smelling and could only be presumed to be a fish, caught then forgotten, several months ago!

Then there was the assortment of odd socks, shirts, and towels to be removed from under the bunks where the oily bilge water had slopped into the canvas storage bags! Once the old contents of the food lockers had been chucked out, they were replaced onto de-gunged shelves by the emergency stores which were brought out as cabin-baggage. Ready for off? No! We are reminded that this is still a teaching week, so don't think you are on holiday!

Passage planning in Palma

Passage planning.

This can be done painlessly from the terrace bar at the Yacht Club before lunch, and it is pointless to hurry because the fuelling jetty does not re-open until after a two hour siesta — if at all. This is mañana territory! When there is no more space left on the table, no-one minds where they sail to. "Heads we turn right, tails we go left."

Weather.

The only official weather report we found was three days old, the Sunday paper gave a vague outlook for the whole Mediterranean, and the Harbour-master gave an indifferent shrug as if to say "What do you want to know that for?" Perhaps the pine cones are the most reliable.

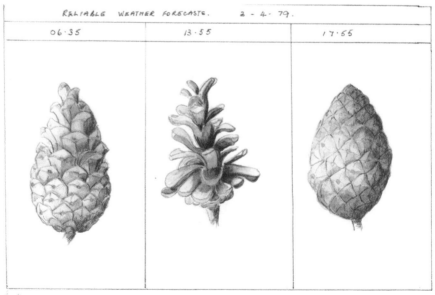

RELIABLE WEATHER FORECASTS. 2 - 4 - 79.

| 06·35 | 13·55 | 17·55 |

Tidal Calculations - Pt. Gross

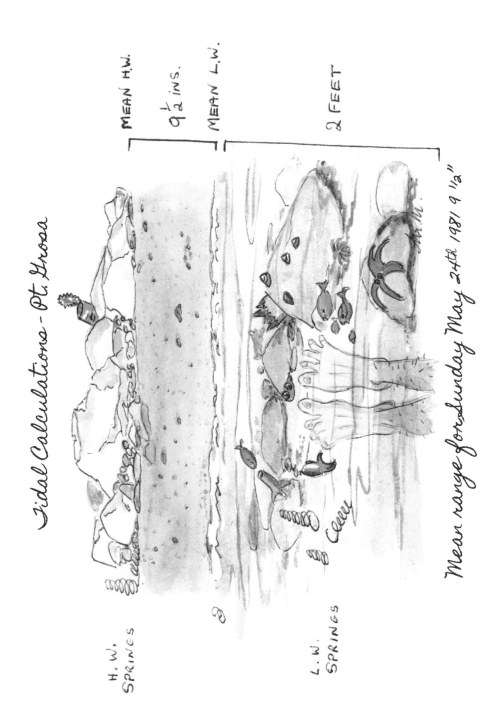

MEAN H.W.

$9\frac{1}{2}$ INS.

MEAN L.W.

2 FEET

H.W. SPRINGS

L.W. SPRINGS

Mean range for Sunday May 24th 1981 9 ½"

Pilotage.

A few carefully selected local postcards will give as much detail as needed of harbours, marinas, and Calas. Although these do not show the bottom of the harbours, the bedsteads, shopping trolleys, and prams are clearly visible amongst the rocks by the harbour wall as the water is so clear.

Anchoring.

"See that pale green patch between two blue bits? There!"

Man overboard drill.

This is more interesting carried out with real men and prevents loss of fenders.

Tidal calculations.

What tide? Mean range — 9"

Navigation.

"Where's West?"

"Dunno, follow these dolphins!"

Much of the pleasure of these weeks lies in the many different personalities you are thrown together with. The typical ratio was two ladies to four men, a good combination which ensured that the girls got plenty of time for sunbathing whilst the men attended to sails, anchors, warps, cooking, deck-scrubbing, and other play.

On the first trip was Mark, referred to as 'Our starboard hand buoy' being young enough to be in the miseries of cutting a wisdom tooth, a sore throat, and pining for his girlfriend. My bunk-mate was also love-lorn, but kept

Assisted passages

"The dolphins will show us the way."

... Loosely translated as "Clear off!"

herself fully occupied by changing her perfume from *Miss Dior* to *Chanel No. 5* to enter a port, or repainting her finger nails to put up the spinnaker. In spite of having to apply another shade of lipstick, she always beat me to the warps and fenders and then disappeared below to reappear a few minutes later with a different hair-style and a tray of canapés which always met with approval, but did nothing for my self-esteem. Her multiple Schnapps-downing also was unrivalled!

Entering Cala Figuera, our skipper, Bill, discounted the wall which had "YATES" roughly daubed across it in red paint. Assuming it to be an advertisement for a well-known wine lodge he chose to make fast on the fisherman's quay on the other side instead, then gave his crew permission to go and mingle with the geriatric sight-seeing coach party on shore. From the terrace, shortly after we had scrounged some bread from the bar, we became aware of a disturbance down near the jetty, and there saw Cap Blanco motoring round and round in the harbour. Our anxious looking skipper and someone were hurling unpleasantries and gestures at each other.

Our 220 yard sprint and long-jump was applauded by the coach-party and spectators, then we learnt that this self-appointed, pseudo-official attendant had been demanding ship's papers and documents and becoming very excitable. As the tirade was loosely translated as "Clear off!" — We did.

In the lively breeze, the spinnaker was ordered up and down like a Yo-Yo until a freak gust caused a spectacular broach. Not many boats sport seaweed on their crosstrees, nor do they have someone not admitting to cleating off both sail-

Barbeque at Cala Del Ras

sheets together!

On another week there was Nan, who woke up only for food and drink, with her husband, Mac, a keen photographer, giving everyone and everything a 100th at F8.

The two youngish 'blades' combed their hair on each tack, and put on clean shirts to disappear in a cloud of *Hi Karate* at each mooring and not returning until 4 a.m.

Full details of these sorties are not known, but you don't get 10% discount at the corner Boutique by just "taking a walk on the headland" even if you do smell lovely!

Cala del Ras looked the perfect cove for our Barbeque. The dinghy sagged under its gastronomic load as it was pushed along by a formation team of swimmers. Collecting firewood is thirsty work. The señora at the beach-bar had watched with interest, but waited until the last beer drained before saying "No fires!" The two lads comb their hair winsomely, and she relents, as long as we go up onto the rocks.

The downturn of that little party came as Sam manoeuvred neatly stern-to into the marina at Cala D'or and picked up a loose mooring line with the propeller. The smirking attendant was not into bribery and ran off shouting "El Capitano!" Sam spent an unsavoury hour diving to free it with a blunt carving-knife, while his helpful crew offer condolences and suggestions that bellows *per rectum* might assist his breathing! Mac gave him 100th at F8.

On another cruise was Rosie, who insisted on making bread on deck whilst sailing but was adamant about being on the tack providing maximum sun for the rising dough. A few arguments arose between navigator, helmsman, and those in defence of the bread. Changing course a few times with the lee-rail under soon made a quagmire of batter on

Boat handling - navigation

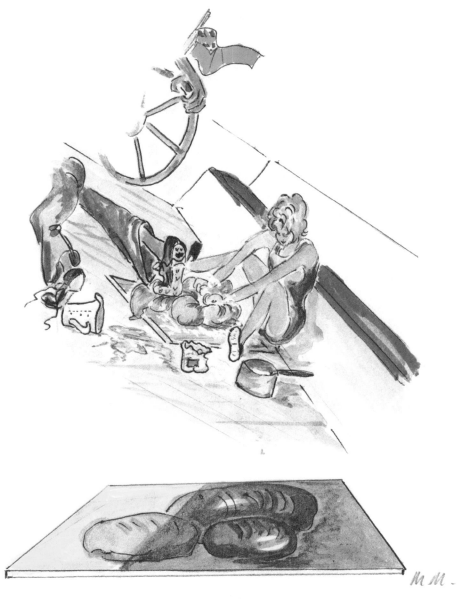

Change course to 060° to get the
sun on rising bread

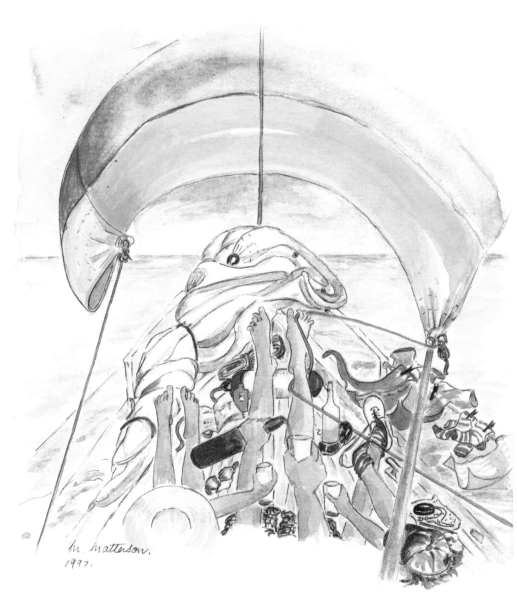

Taking frequent running fixes in Mallorca

the deck, but they do say that she got three buns in the oven on a racing tack!

Our skipper Don, was very technical, precise, and usually right, but I did have a slight altercation with him over the wording in the Pilot book. We were looking for a marina described as a 'Small Yacht harbour' and he wished to go for it. Sailing at 6kts. about 2 miles off, it was clearly visible through the binoculars but I commented that the masts inside it did not look very tall. "It could mean it's a SMALL YACHT harbour.

"No, it's a SMALL yacht harbour, so it's not very big." explained Don. The closer we drew, the more doubtful I became.

"You could be wrong, Skip!"

"No I'm not, you wait." As we surfed towards it, the argument was solved — Bump, Bump, Bump!

"Well, whadaya know? It's a SMALL YACHT harbour!"

Then there was Harry. Harry was really quite charming, but the trouble with Harry was... endless. He was a walking (and limping) disaster! He arrived with a badly swollen, angry septic thumb. Within two hours at sea he had deep lobster-coloured, "don't touch me" sunburn, but insisted on helping to chop the vegetables for dinner, whereupon managed to slice his finger also. We ministered to all his sore parts whilst he yelled loudly.

Passage planning this week was influenced by Harry's quest for a rare species thought to inhabit these islands — the topless waitress! Unluckily, he next tripped over a cleat, painfully stubbing his big toe as he rushed to grab the binoculars when sailing into the next Cala. To his disappointment, it only revealed two caves full of Hippies, a

A few of the 'beautiful people'
at Los Incognitos - Ibiza.

camper's barbeque, and a bar with waiter service.

The limp that he had adopted, impeded his new survey which, from today, dominated most of his waking hours, i.e. "Where is the nearest toilet — quick?" so we had to form a recognisance party to save him time and dignity. On an emergency dash to the back premises of El Corsario he was so impressed with the facilities that he persuaded us to stay for lunch, which seriously depleted the drinks kitty but justified his other visits and saved on leg power.

That evening, two strong crew held him still while I released the pounding pressure in his septic thumb with a boiled-up sail needle. The desire for the topless waitress waned temporarily. So to cheer him up some wag suggested a night sail to Ibiza instead! What happened to priorities chaps?

The light breeze on departure stiffened enough to require a change down to a working jib, Harry and Alec went forward, Alec returned. Fifteen minutes later, Harry was still up there trying to tie his Bowline. By now, skipper was becoming rather irate and gave an in-depth lecture on Bowlines to us all. Harry blamed it on his heavily bandaged thumb and forefinger, but was later said to be tying bowlines round everything and anything.

The old town of Ibiza was interesting. Lured by the exotic dresses of the ladies seen on a terrace bar, the men insisted on climbing up a hundred steps in order to ogle from an adjacent table. It took almost half a pint to realise that these lovely ladies were not female and we had blundered upon a very gay scene!

Rosie's bread had now slowed down Harry's galloping stomach enough to re-continue his original quest once back in Palma, he ordered a taxi and requested that we were to be taken to a place of entertainment. The taxi driver dropped us off at a most dubious-looking dive with the assurance that there were Flamenco dancers, cabaret, and a Disco. He was right, except that he did not mention that, once again, all the 'ladies' were men, and many of the scenes would certainly not have been approved of by Mary Whitehouse and our mothers! In the Disco we flung ourselves with abandon in the gloom to the decibels of *I will survive* and *Y.M.C.A.*

The de-briefing back at *Club Nautico* next day took several bottles, by which time no-one was quite sure what they had learnt this week in accordance with R.Y.A. requirements, but it was most certainly educational last night!

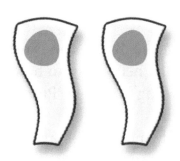

Chapter Eleven

Up the Pole

Flags.

Working through the syllabus, you will have to learn the International Code of Signals, although Morse is not now required. Each boat should be equipped with a complete set of mildewed flags stored somewhere out of reach.

The yellow 'Q' flag will be the one most likely to be used, so may not be in the set but in an unknown 'safe', handy place. This one used to be raised when arriving into a foreign port and told the authorities that you were not badly diseased and had not brought the poodle with you. They could then decide whether to bother to come and see you or not.

On arriving back in England, due to some ancient maritime law, it meant that all wines and spirits must have been consumed before making land-fall — or so I was told!

The purpose of flag and shape recognition is so that you tell what the larger vessels are up to, and might save having to alter course for a tanker which is actually at anchor, but they are not going to care about your intentions. As long as you are not in their way, it is of no interest if you hoist the 'X' flag, to say "Stop carrying out your intentions and watch for my signals" or 'K' — "I wish to communicate with you" because, neither the container-ship nor *Oriana* will be coming over for a chat.

Lights.

On a night passage, recognising the lights can save arguments when trying to convince the helmsman to hold his course between vessels 'pair-trawling' or using 'Purse-Seine' gear.

Military exercises in the middle of Lyme bay will present a display of lights that give rise to interesting guesses but baffles the most knowledgeable, until you hear the gunfire.

Rules of the road.

Learn these well, as you may not often have time to look at the book if a quick decision has to be made. It does not necessarily mean the rules can always be adhered to, for example, it is to neither vessel's advantage to shout "WATER!" to the Japanese freighter which is coming from the wrong direction whilst you are crossing the shipping lanes in the channel. You can try shouting about his dubious parentage if it makes you feel better, but one and two fingered signals are not in the book, therefore not nautical etiquette.

Rope-work.

Knots. You may be able to impress a few others by demonstrating your ability to tie a bowline in your pocket, but you will be subject to a few funny looks rather than applause, so just practise getting it right round a mooring ring or cleat. That will be more useful and won't give you a bad name.

All other basic knots you should know by now, although I did read somewhere that you must have the ability to 'pass a stopper' — don't ask!

Splicing.

A frayed nylon warp can be sealed with a match or on the cooker, but the hairy monster that frays everyone's temper too, must have a proper back-splice or be whipped and sooner or later you will be required to do this — without the hand-book or anyone to prompt you!

Crew 'helping' to free a fouled warp - Cala d'Or

Code flag 'A' - I have a diver down. Keep Clear

I am on Fire. Keep well clear of me

J

You should stop your vessel instantly

L

"It means he is pra(C)tique-ly free
from infection!"

Q

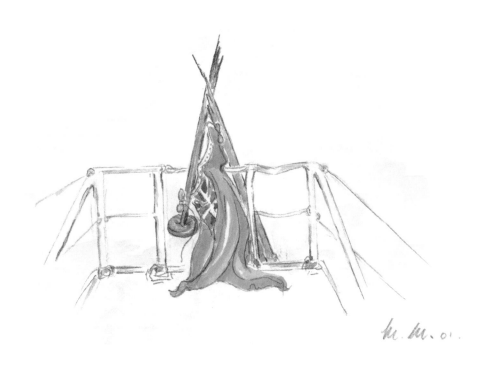

S ▮

My engine (has been) running astern
        is

T

Keep clear of me.
I am engaged in pair trawling

*" What a bloody stupid
place to put a throttle ! "*

U

You are running into danger

I require a tug

Z

M. Matterson.
2001.

*The last step, or more tidal
(mis)calculations
- Newton Ferrers*

Chapter Twelve

The Last Step

The time came for Sam to take the Yachtmaster examinations, which he passed, telling me not to worry as the Oral examiner was a comfortable Yorkshireman so I should get on well with him.

Our son, Paul, after passing his Practical exam, took off with his wife for sixteen months to the Mediterranean in *Trianti*, a 1960's Trintella sloop, leaving as what we considered to be mere children, and returning as adults.

Then it was my turn. I boarded my allocated 36 foot Moody at Hamble, together with the skipper, four burly wags for Coastal 1. Assessment, and the other much younger lady, an overzealous Civil Servant also taking the Yachtmaster's Practical. I shared the large aft cabin with her and her swot books.

With barely time to stow the edibles, we were on a rough overnight passage to Cherbourg, which no-one had knowingly, or willingly, planned.

The reward for this was a day in Cherbourg and a meal out at *Nora Batty's*. After the third night-cap, back on the boat, the conversation took a highly intellectual twist, all about molecules and how objects were not really there, only in the mind. Geoff, a blunt kind of chap, had been a bit puzzled about this, "D'yer mean ter say I'm the only one as can see that Bl--y table and can any of yer see our skipper or

Carol, they're molecules?" Looking round, it slowly dawned that no-one else had seen them for a while either, not since he started the argument! Perhaps on deck with a cigarette we thought.

"I'm going to bed anyway, it's my big day tomorrow, they'll turn up later. Goodnight lads." Feeling the way down the narrow, dark walkthrough to the aft cabin, I fell head-long over something soft and bulky — someone had left a sail-bag out, I thought.

On dragging it out into the light, it proved to be my sleeping-bag! It took a minute to accept why, as that situation does not normally happen on board in our sailing fraternity. "You do know now that you won't pass tomorrow, Don't you, Monica?" quipped the lads!

The saloon table made an uncomfortable bed, but I did not have the courage to bang on the cabin door and demand my rightful place, so the next morning, I was not at my shining best and ached in every joint.

The following morning, dreading the embarrassment of the appearance of the errant pair, the down to earth Geoff volunteered to take down two mugs of tea, and, banging loudly on the door shouted – "What a Bl--y skipper, can't even navigate his way to his own Bl--y bunk!!"

The young lady apologised to me and wished me luck, but that was not much consolation for the tortured night. I was twitchy, skipper was going to be watching my every move and monitoring every command, so I could not afford to feel queasy today. In spite of never having been prone to sea-sickness, I decided to play it safe, and took half of a tablet of the kind reputed not to cause drowsiness.

Far too early I was prowling the pontoon watching the

wind direction, deciding which spring to take off first and what else I must do before leaving Cherbourg for the passage to Bray on the island of Alderney.

The wind was a south-easterly Force 4-5, a little lumpy with good visibility, but right from taking off the wrong spring first, it was obvious that I had not "put the right chip in for memory"!

Coming out of the harbour I just caught sight of a red buoy sneaking past on the wrong side, since so far, I had omitted to give the helmsman any directions presuming that he would know about buoyage!

Once out of the Grande Rade, the skipper asked me what course I wished the helm to make, and thinking only in terms of "turn left and follow the coast as usual", I had not actually considered putting it into numbers. A quick glance at the chart fortuitously showed a course-line printed with 120 degrees, compass right where we were. "Great, - steer 120C!" I instructed the helm.

A moment later — "Psst, Monica," he whispered, "if I do that it takes me round in a circle and back into Cherbourg!"

"For goodness sake get your brain into gear." I told myself, and gave him a quick reciprocal course, hoping that the *about face* swerve would go unnoticed.

Becoming more relaxed now, I thought I would flaunt my bit of authority and give the rest of the crew a few running fixes to play at, then went below to check them on the chart as we approached Cap de la Hague. The chart came up closer and closer until it hit me in the face! How long I was sprawled asleep across the chart table I have no idea, but I oozed back to reality to the sound of the skipper bawling, nay screaming, loudly, "MONICA!! Come up here at once

"Come up here!"

and LOOK where you are!" I had only seen the Alderney Race once before and had thought it impressive and rather awesome, but this time the boat was being dragged down sideways - and it was my fault!

Now thoroughly awake, we put the engine on full throttle and slowly clawed a way out and safely into Bray harbour. My crew were most kind and sympathetic, which helped to buffer the skipper's scathing remarks.

I did take the exam again, but without the tablets and more success, perhaps it was because the next skipper did not bark at me.

Instead, he quietly made polite requests that you knew had to be taken seriously. "Now dear, would you mind picking up that buoy then sailing off it again, when you are ready!"

Subtle hints were made that, Fred (an amiable fellow lured out of retirement as extra ballast) had run out of his panatelas, so it would be most kind if I could anchor in Totland bay and row him ashore to get some more. "We'll go to Guernsey early tomorrow, so perhaps you can work out the tides now whilst we sail backwards till the tide turns, then take us to Poole tonight!"

The dark clouds I noticed ahead near the Needles were diagnosed as FOG, so my calculations were all in vain. Yarmouth was a familiar retreat. The week passed by in such a laid back and genteel manner that I forgot that I was under close scrutiny but had obviously performed well enough to earn his certificate.

Time is now passing all too quickly towards your final examination, the R.Y.A. Yachtmaster Oral and there is everything to be revised that you have supposedly learnt in the last two or three years. Rules of the road, Lights, and buoyage. Navigation — can you still remember how to do a Running Fix? Flags and Signals, and how long ago is it since you needed to do an Eye-Splice or whipping? "Oh, it seems endless."

The date and time was duly arranged for a few of us to face this exam, and I thought that I was as well prepared as possible while sitting on a hard, splintered chair in a cold, dreary corridor — waiting.

From the moment I heard this clipped voice proclaiming "No! - if I want a cup of coffee, I'll get it myself." it occurred to me that he did not sound like the 'comfortable Yorkshireman' that Sam had mentioned. My only bit of self-confidence dropped down its first notch.

The weather chart that I created from his rapidly recited forecast must have been acceptable because he grunted. With a blunt pencil and wonky parallels, my navigation vector was as accurate as a shaking hand would allow, but I felt his vibes telling me I was not quick enough.

Next came a series of questions on chart symbols, and out of twenty, got stuck on one of the Aero-beacons and a devious type of sea-bed. Not wishing to appear cowed by this, I was bold enough to suggest that when on the boat, I would look it up in the book if I wasn't sure!

There was a discernible draft as the pale blue, shiny book came through the air, and skated across the table to halt in front of me. I shot him a glance of acknowledgement!

Then came the Morse code, both sending and receiving, fortunately no longer needed for examination purposes. This was going well, considering it was a page of some obscure narrative poem in old English, but one slight hesitation towards the end, and I had to start from the beginning again! My next glance was meant to be a plea for mercy, but by then I suspected that he did not approve of ladies aspiring to be skippers, so was not going out of his way to be helpful.

A hairy piece of rope that would have disgraced a scarecrow's trousers then came sliding across the table to me along with the challenge "Put a back-splice in THAT!" implying "If you can!" I did, and slid it back with the hint of a glint of defiance.

A barrage of questions then followed, mostly reasonable and answered with renewed confidence, perhaps we are at last on the same wavelength! Wrong! I tripped up badly on two that I considered just a bit sneaky. One was about light recognition and could not work it out, but the answer he wanted was akin to two Minesweepers pair-trawling.

If the other question had been worded differently then, perhaps, maybe? "How would you launch a Life-raft?" No problem, I thought, and gave him what I took to be a fairly good account, right up to climbing into it, then hoped for a glimmer of approval. He was evidently not satisfied and said "No, your Life-raft is still sitting there unopened!"

"Right," I replied, "then I'd give the rope another sharp tug." I hopefully suggested.

"No, it still hasn't opened!"

"Give it a harder pull then!" He was becoming a little peevish, it must be nearly lunch-time. I was getting desperate; I could not imagine what he wanted me to say, after yet again, he said it had still not opened. "Alright, I give up!"

It transpired that his question should have been translated

as, "How long is a piece of string" and I hadn't thought to find out how many yards to a Life-raft, Now if he had wanted to know how to immobilise a water-spout (shoot it!) or how to keep whales from ramming your boat, I could have told him — but he didn't ask!

It came as no surprise that I did not pass the Oral examination, but a slight disappointment to learn that, the next candidate he tested lost his cool and shouted at him. Because this was seen to be assertiveness, he passed — just. If only I had known, I most certainly could have shouted instead of trying to appear unflappable.

We later learnt that this was the examiner for the Merchant Navy, so I could possibly have qualified to be an officer on a coaster as well as a 32 foot yacht.

Enough courage for a re-sit was never mustered, but it has not been at all detrimental to the many subsequent years of happy sailing in many different cruising grounds and weather conditions.

The process of learning is never ending. When you finally have all the necessary pages in your Log Book ticked and signed, that is really just the beginning. Have fun whilst recalling that:-

"He who goes to sea for pleasure,
would go to hell for a pastime!"

About the Author

Monica Matterson was born in 1926 in Hunmanby, a village near Filey on the north Yorkshire Coast, moving to Filey in 1935. After Primary School, attended the Bridlington High School for Girls, travelling daily by steam train. From 1942 to 1944 trained at the Adela Shaw Orthopaedic Hospital in Kirby Moorside before three and a half years at Scarborough Hospital to become a State Registered Nurse. A further six months Midwifery was undertaken at Leamington Spa before marrying Sam in 1950 and living in Coalville Leicestershire where the interest in sailing began after rearing two sons. She moved down to Bursledon after Sam's retirement to be nearer to the boat, and thence to Hamble-le-Rice in Hampshire where she is now living.

Also by Monica Matterson

978-1-908387-92-9 (Paperback)
978-1-908387-95-0 (Hardback)

"Although a originally intended for three Grandsons, I hope many others can enjoy and relate to the reminiscences of a childhood and the simplicity of a Yorkshire village life in the 1920's and 30's"

Set against a background of change before, during and after World War II, this book chronicles the author's life and illustrations from early childhood to the present day.

Life was so much different in those days - would you let your daughter hitch-hike on lorries, climb out of the window of a moving train, or climb a flagpole on the Nurse's home roof? Only if you didn't know about it!

Lightning Source UK Ltd.
Milton Keynes UK
UKOW06f1814140615

253459UK00011B/45/P